# VICTORY

## Vignettes

## & Voices

Glory Fagan

Victory Vignettes & Voices

Copyright © 2024 by Glory Fagan

All rights reserved.

Contact the author at glorywritertype@gmail.com

ISBN 9798879151053

Cover Illustration by Cathy Green

Cover design by Dr. Amanda Williams

In beloved memory and grateful appreciation of those who
inspired this book

Prelude

This book is a work of fiction with facts woven in. First and
foremost, the musical theme uniting the stories is inspired by historical
fact. During World War II, Steinway and Sons, best known for their
magnificent grand pianos, were, due to a scarcity of materials,
forbidden by the War Department from manufacturing pianos. To
continue to stay in business and with a work force suddenly comprised
of more women than ever, the storied piano company retooled their
output and produced gliders and caskets. The gliders were for troop
transport and built like giant wooden model airplanes, shipped
unassembled in huge crates to be assembled overseas. They were
sometimes referred to as Flying Coffins due to a greater than average
likelihood of fatality. The caskets were, obviously and sadly enough, for
dead soldiers.

The Steinway family, however, thought it preferable to produce
something that would benefit the living. Knowing how universally
essential music was and is to boost morale, the company proposed
making pianos for delivery and use by soldiers and sailors in every
theater of the war. At first the plan met with resistance from the
powers that be: "Steinways —arguably the best piano ever made—for
servicemen?" Their rebuttal was something along the lines of, you send
them the best wool socks, don't you? Why would you knowingly
provide anything but the best?

Still the best had to be practical and meet certain guidelines of the War Production Board. These Steinways weighed a fraction of the originals and contained a tenth of the copper, nickel, and brass of conventional pianos. Yet they had 88 keys and were sturdy little instruments that four men could carry and move. Modifications were made for the various climates for which they were intended. They not only had to be well-constructed, but the pianos also needed to be shipped in crates that made them impervious to damage, especially as some would actually be parachuted to their final destination. What's more, the pianos needed to be painted certain colors. Olive Drab Government Issue (ODGI) pianos, for example, were intended for the Army, while those lacquered blue or gray were outfitted for naval vessels. Nearly 2,500 upright pianos were produced between 1942 until 1953, the year of the Korean armistice. Crated and shipped with tuning tools and sheet music, pianos were delivered to every continent.

These G.I. upright field pianos cost under $500 to produce, but their value was inestimable. Music professor and pianist Garik Pedersen from the University of Michigan is the country's foremost authority responsible for bringing to light this little-known project Steinway called Victory Verticals. Pedersen tells the story of one personified piano, W672, that became a casualty of war and subsequently received a posthumous Purple Heart and a Silver Star for gallantry after receiving damage from a wayward Japanese bomb!

*"While Hitler's Army sang for political reasons, U.S. forces sang about God, loss, love and country."~ Garik Pedersen*

During the first half of the twentieth century, pianos were more ubiquitous than bathtubs in American homes and nearly everyone could play, either by notes or by ear, or at the least, they could sing. Having access to a piano allowed those in the armed services an escape from their circumstances and provided a reminder of just what they were fighting for. The piano allowed for a level playing field. Those from every demographic and ethnic background carried with them thoughts of home when they played or sang. The sheet music packed with the Victory Verticals reflected the diverse musical tastes of their audiences. Ranging from the patriotic and spiritual to the sacred and syncopated, whether played by trained U.S.O. musicians or amateur soldiers and sailors, the music played by enlisted and officers alike entertained themselves and others under every conceivable condition and circumstance from middle C. The sounds of home gave audiences a sense of home. Boogie woogie, jazz, and swing raised their spirits. Anthems and hymns lifted their souls, and cinematic scores and hit parade numbers moved their feet.

It is against this rich soundtrack that our stories are set. As a matter of fact, I created an **Amazon playlist** of 40s songs and a **YouTube video playlist** to accompany the book. Most tunes will probably be familiar to you, but you might want to give a listen, especially to unfamiliar ones, to better appreciate the story. (**https://amzn.to/48hHB8d** & **http://bit.ly/Victory-Vertical** ) You won't be surprised to understand why 40s Junction on Sirius radio is one of my favorite presets.

Although the actual Vertical Victory project is grounded in historical fact, the balance of the book is constructed of myth, legend, and anecdote. For they are the stories, real and imagined, of people who shared with me their fathers' and their grandfathers' and even their mothers' and grandmothers' tales. By and large though, the stories of The Greatest Generation were not always verbalized. They came to us second-hand or only after a loved one died, when medals were unearthed, and newspaper accounts were uncovered. I asked friends and family to share insight into the stories of their veterans, and they trusted me to weave those details into fiction. As my story needed to be peopled, the characters you will meet are composites drawn from details and drafted from the DNA of their descendants. I hope you recognize yourself in the shadows.

The result is the book you are now reading. Herein lie traces of the World War II vets even among our family, namely my maternal grandfather, my mom's beloved stepdad, and my husband's dad. Mom still has the tiny pewter tea set and a watercolor of cornflowers from Paris, and a little pair of Dutch clogs that her dad brought from overseas for her. My husband has a silk map and a 48-star flag from his father's time in Hawaii, plus a cigar box of miscellaneous artifacts that includes the funeral program for a fellow townsman killed in the South Pacific.

Mark Twain admonished in *Huckleberry Finn*, "Persons attempting to find a motive in this narrative will be prosecuted; persons attempting to find a moral in it will be banished; persons attempting to find a plot in it will be shot." The same applies here. Told as a series of vignettes followed by voices (perhaps ironically written in present tense), the book begins in December and moves through a succession of months, though not necessarily falling in the same year. Some of the characters are separated by mere degrees, and you will encounter them again. Others stand alone. Like the actual people upon which they are based, all characters, who appear in varying shades of fabrication, are as acquainted with music as with air, so specific songs are associated with each.

It bears noting that this remains primarily a work of fiction. Names, characters, places, and incidents are (generally) products of the author's imagination and are used fictitiously. Occasional resemblance to actual events or locales or persons, living or dead, might be unintentional, but then again, it might be because it is entirely true. Only those who contributed information will likely recognize if a scenario has been inspired by their family. It's up to each individual if he or she wants to suggest the correlation between a character and his or her forebear. A few accounts are practically verbatim and directly from the person who served in the war.

I wish to thank the following people, in no particular order, for entrusting me with the stories of their loved ones. Many contributed details and character attributes, several offered wonderful anecdotes, and a *few provided such poignant stories they appear in their entirety. In some case, the stories appear untouched and without name change. Others have narrative embellishment and character development from my feeble imagination. Without their contributions I would not have been able to create something wholly new about victories that came at incalculable cost, arising from the legacies of family members from that greatest of generations.

*SHARON CARROLL
*THE IRWIN FAMILY—
BRENT, KELSEY & JOAN
*JOY SHERARD
*EDD GREEN
*MARK JUSTIN
*TOMMY TAYLOR
JAN SCHWARZ
ROBERT SIGRIST
BETH MOUTRAY
SHEA WORKMAN HENDERSON
MARTHA TAYLOR
CINDY RICHARDSON
PATRICIA KURTZ
LORNA OFFICER
MERLE GREEN
EARL MCKINNEY
JANIE CHRISTENSEN
KEVIN FAGAN
DONNA GAINES
TISHA TAYLOR
NANCY BLACK
BECKY HARROLD

I am indebted to advance readers **Kelsey Irwin**, **Kim Fowler**, and **Ashley Dawson** for their encouragement and constructive feedback, **Cathy Green** for the cover illustration, putting pencil to paper to sketch exactly what I imagined, and **Dr. Amanda Williams** for helping design the cover. **The Story Collective**, the greatest independent bookstore in downtown St. Joseph, helped launch the book into the world. I appreciate the friendships that allow us to support one another in our creative endeavors. And lastly, my husband Kevin, who has read every book ever written about World War II, ate leftovers without complaint more often than not during the writing of this book.

## VIGNETTE ONE

## DECEMBER

### "White Christmas"

His dad never smoked a day in his life, or not that he ever knew of, but Frank kept the cigar box he found among Pop's things on his dresser all the same. He tried not to move it around much because even the slightest shift made the dust on the dresser's glass top more apparent. Frank turned on a lamp in the upstairs bedroom. Under the glass lay a white silk map of the world and a smallish 48-star flag topped by assorted elementary school pictures of his daughter Paige that chronicled her dental history, installments slid under the glass edge with each successive year. Gapped-tooth grins in the early years gave way to braces in middle school and ended with a beautiful, albeit expensive, smile in her senior portrait.

The gallery of school pictures continued in the kitchen where her first few years as a teacher were posted by mismatched magnets. Paige's own daughter Molly's premiere as a preschool student hung beside her mom. The photo depicted a crooked haircut, evidence of a self-inflicted attempt at bangs, but all her baby teeth on full display. Frank had been promised a kindergarten photo the minute they were available.

He knew there was a pair of old wire-framed glasses in the cigar box, and, as he loved his only daughter very much, he was willing to disturb the patina of dust to retrieve them for her classroom pageant as Mrs. Claus or maybe it was Santa himself, he couldn't be sure. He just knew Paige needed an old-fashioned pair of wire-framed glasses as a prop, and he and she both recalled having seen a pair in Pop's cigar box. She was due any moment to pick them up on her way to practice.

Since Paula had passed, the dust had really gotten out of hand. Although, truth be told, Paula was never much of a clean freak herself when it came to dusting. She joked that if you didn't touch or move anything, nobody was the wiser.

A glance out the window into the early evening fading light confirmed that snow was picking up. He picked up the Roi Tan box and lifted the lid, tentatively connected by a torn paper hinge. Christmas music came from the kitchen. Opening it he had a sudden momentary memory of a music box his mother used to have. It played a classical piece; Frank couldn't remember its name. The Alexa device that Paige had given him before Thanksgiving had surprised him with her capability to tell him the weather, amuse Molly with knock knock jokes, and play practically any song. For sound quality, he preferred to listen to the collection of LPs he and Paula had accumulated early in their marriage, but Alexa certainly was handier, especially as Paige had set him up with a holiday playlist. He stood and listened for a bit, cradling the box so as not to damage the lid any further.

Frank wasn't all that keen on whoever Wham was so was glad when "Last Christmas" ended. This would be his first Christmas without Paula. He didn't have time to get all maudlin, so as Bing began to dream of a White Christmas from the other room, Frank shuffled through a stack of postcards in the cigar box one-handed. Several had interesting old stamps and spidery handwriting, but some just seemed to have been purchased as keepsakes, as they were without postage, cancellation, or writing of any kind.

Sidetracked from his quest for antique spectacles by the array of cardstock depicting variously Kansas City's Union Station, a black and white desert landscape with a fake-looking jackalope, Judy Garland's colorized Bel Air mansion in California, and assorted Ma and Pa Kettle penny postcards, Frank thumbed through the stack. Balancing the box, he turned each card over to see who might have sent the ones with writing and when. Several seemed to have arrived sometime in the late '40s. He marveled at the two- cent stamps.

Most of the ones that had made their way through the postal service, five for a dime, were souvenirs from his Uncle Bert, known in the family as Toots, from his days as a traveling trumpet player on the road with a swing band. The messages were practically identical and along the lines of "Hi, folks, wish you were here" whether mailed from Lincoln, Nebraska, or Athens, Georgia. Flipping through postmarks from Fargo to Philly, Frank was amused by Toot's lack of detail, undoubtedly censored for the sake of his grandmother, Cora, who disapproved of Bert's vagabond lifestyle playing in beer joints after he got out of the service.

Frank stopped at a pair of praying hands oriented vertically. It took a beat for Frank to realize that though the dimensions were identical, this was lighter weight and not a postcard at all, but rather a folded memorial service program. He laid the cigar box on the dresser, dust be damned, and set the postcards aside to look at the funeral's order of service. Inside, opposite the twenty-third Psalm, Frank saw that the program was for a Staff Sergeant Ronald F. Eastman, April 4, 1917 - Luzon, January 28, 1945. He had heard of Luzon. In the Philippines, he thought. What also caught his attention was the date of service, March 11, 1945, nearly three months after the date of the Staff Sergeant's death.

After a salute to both the American and Christian flags, a scripture reading, and a congregational hymn, and prayer, the program listed a Chaplain Robert Norman delivering a military memorial service message. A choir from Rosecrans Field, now Rosecrans Air National Guard Base, provided special music.

He certainly recognized the name of the funeral home, as well as that of the man who delivered the eulogy. His mom's family, the Thompsons, had lived on the same block as the funeral home. His mom had been Ginny Thompson before she became a Moss. Though she had died years before his Pop, her sister-in-law still lived in an assisted living apartment not far from him.

He smiled at the mention of The Reverend W.W. Taylor, listed as officiant. Though Frank had never met him, and he had been dead for years, Taylor had been the guy who had presided at his mom and pop's wedding in the early 1950s. Frank knew the preacher had lived in the Baptist parsonage of their small hometown church and had been referred to by most as Brother Billy.

But to Frank's knowledge, there were no Eastmans in the family. He wondered who the Staff Sergeant might have been. And how Pop, who had served in Europe and not the Pacific front, had known him. Frank had never heard an Eastman mentioned. He turned the folded program over to read the obituary, but the page was blank. What happened to Eastman, his next of kin, and the usual biographical details may have been known to those in attendance at the time, practically 80 years ago, but they were a mystery to Frank. Whited out by nothingness.

He heard the stampede of footsteps on the stairs. "There you are, Poppy!" came a voice from the doorway. Molly, shrugging off her coat and pulling off her mittens, ran into the room and threw her arms around his legs. "Looky. I lost a toof," she said, tugging her lower lip down to expose a tiny gap.

"Hi, Pumpkin," Frank said, giving her a peck on the check. Putting Eastman's service brochure next to the cigar box, Frank lifted the girl to his waist. He brushed a few flakes of snow from her hair and reached for the dried-up leather glasses case left in the cigar box, which he knew held a pair of wire-framed glasses.

"Found these," he announced, holding them out to Paige as she entered the room. "They were in Pop's things."

"I knew you would come through," Paige said, taking them from Frank. "I'm sorry we have to run. Molly, give Poppy a hug and put your coat back on." The girl squeezed his neck tightly and then jumped from his arms.

Frank watched from the window as the two made their way through the new fallen snow. He noted the rising moon gave the luster of midday as they made their way to the car and turned to wave. Watching them drive away, Frank decided to go visit his aunt the first chance he had to see if she had any recollection of the man listed in the funeral program.

## Voice One

## DECEMBER 1944, THE PHILIPPINES

### "Chattanooga Choo Choo"

"Hey Sarge, get a look at that piana," the private yells as they enter the dance hall. "We match!" He takes off his hat, wipes his brow, and shoves the folded cap into his back pocket. Dark circles mark the perspiration of his olive drab short-sleeved uniform shirt.

"Believe it or not, it's a Steinway," Staff Sergeant Eastman, tall and lanky and with black hair and wire-rimmed glasses, shouts above the band playing a swing tune.

"It's green. That ain't like any piana I ever seen," the private says, incredulous. "It ain't even black."

"Called a Victory Vertical. Made by Steinway," Eastman shouts. "Government Issue Olive Drab, same as us. All eighty-eight keys. About a tenth of the brass or metal. Otherwise, sounds a lot like the fancier ones. Shoved 'em off a plane and airdropped by parachute," explains Eastman. "Packed in a crate, also in a lovely shade of olive. Had to see one for myself," he adds, mostly to himself.

"Can't believe they sent us Steinways," the private muses. "All the way over here. I took lessons from an old lady at church. Hated to practice though."

"Supposedly some of the brass resisted, but relented when Steinway asked if they would send the best or the worst wool sock to troops. Same principle. War department decided to ship these plain jane-GI pianos all over the world. The factory treats these Victory Verticals they call them for insects and humidity, hell, everything but malaria. Some delivered by plane, some by train," the Sergeant explains.

"But all arrive by trucks and Jeeps in the same basic Army-approved color, I bet," the private suggests. "Didn't Henry Ford say you could get a Model T in any color you want, as long as it was black?"

Eastman laughs. "True, but not the Navy ones," Eastman replies. "Bet you can't guess what color they are."

"You gotta be kiddin' me. Seasick gray?"

"All except those that are blue," Eastman laughs. "They were installed on subs during construction while they were still in dry dock. They'll have a helluva time getting them out after the war."

"No sh*t!" laughs the private, shaking his head. "Oh, sorry, sir. Pardon my French."

Eastman waves him off, and he, the private, and a corporal thread their way through the sea of olive camo to three open chairs at a table in the back of the room.

Though it's December, the heat is stifling even with the windows open. "I'm thirsty. Gonna get us some beers," the quiet corporal says, on recon to find the bar. "Save my seat."

The private pulls a red and white pack of cigarettes from his uniform pockets and pats himself down for matches but comes up short. Eastman hands him a small box. The private strikes, draws on the Winston, and exhales "Thanks, Sarge. Want one?"

Eastman shakes his head, reaches in his pocket, and unwraps a cigar. He smells it and spits the end onto the floor. Cheeks work to ignite the Roi Tan and the sergeant tosses the match. No one in this all-male fraternity of soldiers is dancing as the swing number comes to an end. The piano player gathers his music, and four band members, a short saxophone player, a trumpet player, a chubby clarinetist, and a tall trombonist, grab hold of the piano on stage and lower it to the dance floor. They lift it with ease, as if it were a Formica kitchen table rather than a heavy upright piece of musical furniture. Under the watchful eye of their drummer, whose services are unneeded for the task, they leave the dull green piano front and center and retreat for a smoke break and a drink.

Eastman picks up the earlier conversation as if he had been thinking of it all along. "The government shut Steinway down. Wouldn't let them make pianos on account they take so much metal, so they got a contract building wooden gliders, kinda like model airplanes, and even coffins, which came in handy. Got 'em thinking about how to pack a piano in a box," Eastman puffs on his cigar. "Buddy of mine said they approached Roosevelt for permission to build pianos again to boost troop morale. Had to meet a bunch of bureaucratic rigmarole but hear tell they've shipped them all over the place."

The crowd, only moments ago tapping their feet to the beat or ignoring the tune entirely as their laughter was drowned out by the music, grows restless. The corporal joins his officer and hands him a beer. The private looks disappointed. "Only got two hands, numbnuts," the taciturn corporal explains. The private drifts off on his own to seek out the bar. "Gonna see a man about a horse," he says as he leaves.

"You got a girl back home?" Eastman asks the corporal, making conversation as he watches the smoke from the cigar ascend.

"Wife," he replies, minimally holding up his end of the dialogue. "And a daughter. You?"

"Yes, a fiancé. Virginia."

"That where you're from?" the corporal inquires, positively chatty.

"Oh, no, no, that's her name, Virginia. Sweet gal. I'm from Missouri," Eastman adds, pronouncing it *Missour-ah*. The two men run out of things to say and drink in silence.

Eventually a uniformed soldier unfolds and takes a seat on a wooden folding chair, sets a sheet of music above the keyboard, and runs his fingers across the keys. The mass of men continue to stir in the tropical humidity. The man riffs a medley of upbeat church tunes, throwing in a few bars from "When the Saints Come Marching In" with "Onward Christian Soldiers," but his listeners mostly tune out his sacred selection, except for one guy who shouts, "Goodnight Irene," whether as a suggestion or in exasperation, no one can be sure, but it draws a laugh.

Undeterred, the man at the keyboard continues to play with only the Staff Sergeant as a silent participant in a dueling piano duet. Oblivious to the corporal sitting in silence beside him and his beer largely untouched, Eastman moves his hands in concert with the piano player, drumming his fingers on his uniformed thighs out of sight under the table. He hums the last line, "With the cross of Jesus going on before." A weak round of applause greets the song's conclusion, whether for musicianship or the song's conclusion unclear.

The man at the piano stands, loosens his tie, and unaccompanied sings, "Pardon me, boy." Then he bangs out "Chattanooga Choo Choo" to the yelled accompaniment of the audience, "Is that the cat that chewed your new shoes?" Joined after a few bars by his brass bandmates jumping on stage, the guy pounds the government issue celluloid-coated ivories treated especially for tropical conditions, the action board twice baked to resist warping. Staff Sergeant Easton abandons his furtive under table play and begins his silent accompaniment tabletop where there's more room for his long fingers to reach.

Kicking the wooden chair out of the way, the piano player shakes his Army regulation-defying hair and sweat sprays from his brow in rhythm with the boogie woogie beat. The crowd sings and shout the words in varying degrees of inebriation but with enthusiastic unison. A raucous round of genuine clapping, stomping and two-fingered approving whistles begins before the song even ends.

After the ovation and whistles subside, the piano player rights his chair, smooths his hair into place and takes his seat. "Thank you, ladies and gentlemen, or I guess mainly just gents. We're the Jive Bombers. Give a hand for Toots, Jerome, Butch, and Saul on horns and Andy on drums. The boys will be back in five, but now you are in for a real treat."

"Pretty sure I know one of those guys from back home," Eastman volunteers as the crowd claps to no one in particular.

The pianist's brethren disappear into the darkness, and a makeshift spotlight catches a woman in a cream-colored dress stepping out of the shadows. As she approaches the microphone on stage followed by the beacon, to a man, the onlookers settle quietly. A few bars of music later, she begins to sing. "I'm dreaming of a White Christmas, just like the ones I used to know." Sergeant Eastman's hands, poised to play along, fall motionless to his side.

In a month's time, Eastman would be dead.

**VIGNETTE TWO**

**JANUARY**

**"Jeepers Creepers"**

"Hey, do you have number twelve?" the muffled voice came from a man doubled over rifling through a cardboard box filled with old books.

"Which one is that?" the woman asked, not taking her eyes from the row of yellow spines on the shelf before her. She ran her fingers along the numbered series.

"*Message in the Hollow Oak*," came the man's voice.

"Yeah, I have that one," his wife said, pulling one of the books from the shelf for inspection. Number 7, *The Clue in the Diary*, the one with the first appearance by Ned Nickerson.

"It doesn't match your others anyway," he said dismissively. Without realizing it, he began to whistle.

A few seconds passed. "What do you mean?" she asked without looking up from the copy in her hand, her finger marking the 25th and, and in keeping with the whole of the series, final chapter.

"I guess it's one. It's by Carolyn Keene. It's just not yellow," he stops whistling to shout back.

"Carolyn Keene was just the pen name of a series of ghostwriters," the woman replied distractedly.

"Well, whoever she was, that woman was a regular James Patterson," the man said to himself.

"As a matter of fact, a man actually created the character," the woman added, as if hearing her husband's thoughts.

"This one is junk. It isn't even yellow and blue. Wouldn't fit in with your others. It has an old-timey Nancy on the cover with a magnifying glass. There's a bunch of writing inside it. Pretty worthless," he said dismissively, dropping the book back into the box. "It's freezing up here. I'm going to go downstairs and look for a cup of coffee. Take your time."

Resuming his whistling, something catchy but the woman couldn't put a name to it, the man descended the staircase from the new and used bookstore to the bistro below on the first floor. As his wife walked over to the box, a young woman in a "Jo's Second Story Books" sage green sweatshirt and fur-lined boots appeared. She hurriedly lifted the box out of the woman's way. "I'll just move these things. I'm so sorry. They just came in from an estate and I haven't had time to sort them or anything. Sorry they are in the way."

"Mind if I look at one of them?" the woman blurted as the tall green sweatshirt retreated.

"Of course. I mean, I guess. Which one?"

"I . . I'm not sure," the woman answered, barely registering the young woman's quizzical expression. "That old one on top, I think."

"Okay, I'll just set them here and let you look," said the young woman, the eponymous Jo the woman guessed, setting the box on the counter, and pulling her auburn hair back off her shoulders. The woman nodded her thanks, vaguely recognizing the book seller's eye color was the same sage green as her shirt. The melody to "Jeepers Creepers," the song her husband had been whistling, popped in her head and she began to hum "Where'd you get those eyes?" to hide her excitement at the prospect of finding a first edition.

Spotting a volume with a blue gray cloth cover with orange lettering and the silhouette of a girl, the woman snatched up the book her husband had discarded.

"Oh wow, I hadn't noticed that one," Jo said, returning.

"I actually collect the classic yellow ones," the woman mused, acting disinterested as she thumbed through the old book, her heart racing.

"My mom read every single one of them when she was a girl," Jo volunteered. "My grandma kept her in constant supply. She was a librarian," she laughed, "so Mom kind of had an in. Got first dibs before they were even cataloged. Grandma only let her read a new book as long as she could do so in two days. So it was available for circulation to library patrons. Everybody else got it for two weeks. Made mom a fast reader but the first one to get her hands on a copy."

"I always wished my dad was like Carson Drew," the woman stated, wanting to steer clear of any discussion of the book. "He let her go gallivanting all over River Heights in her little blue roadster, solving mysteries with Bess and George," the woman said with a wry smile. "Plus, they had a housekeeper."

"Grandma always tried to get me to read them," Jo said. "I always intended to read them. I'd be better at running this bookstore if I had listened to half the things she said. I read all the time as a kid though, but regretfully, more along the lines of *Babysitters Club* and *Goosebumps*," she laughed. "You know, classic literature."

"My daughter read those too," the woman sighed dramatically, before suddenly becoming all business. "I'd like to take this one. It's got a bunch of writing all over it," she announced abruptly. "How much?" The woman looked away in hopes the girl wouldn't know the value of the first edition.

"You know, I really don't think I can part with it just yet," the young woman with the sage eyes said decisively and gently reached for the book. The woman held onto the faded cloth covered book for several seconds before handing it back to Jo.

Jo continued, "Like I said, it just came in from an estate. The lady had no known family or living relatives. It's not even in the system. I'm really sorry. I should have saved you the trouble."

The woman turned to join her husband downstairs for a latte, and Jo gently carried the book to the check-out desk. She flipped through pages and stopped at a first black and white illustration with teenage girls, one fashionably dressed and the other in dungarees, trying to stay upright in the interior of an overturning sleeper car. Jo read the caption, "Nancy staggered to her feet and looked about her for Bess and George." She sat down and skimmed to the end the chapter just as the amateur sleuth and her friends found themselves, along with fellow passengers, in mortal peril. Jo decided she would read the book from the beginning, knowing her mother and grandmother would be proud.

She turned back to the front cover. It really didn't look like the iconic Nancy Drews she had lined up with the distinctive yellow spines. Turning to the title page, Jo noted the writing the woman had mentioned. It was a series of inscriptions by what appeared to be two different hands on the end sheets. In what Jo sensed was a man's writing, the printed notation in black ink said, "To Hannah. From AJ. September 1944."

Then below that, in a larger childish cursive script the words "From Hannah. To AJ. October 1944" was penciled.

Again in the man's hand, this time more hurried and in pencil, a third line read, "From AJ. To Glynis. Maybe next time."

**VOICE TWO**

**JANUARY 1945, BELGIUM**

**"Two Cigarettes in the Dark"**

"What are you reading there, Soldier," the nurse on duty of the Evac Hospital asks the newly admitted man with the elevated leg as she makes her rounds.

"Just a book my kid sister gave me," Novak says, sheepishly tucking the book with the blue cover under the wool blanket. "It's too dark to read anyway."

"What's it about?" the nurse asks. She checks the field dressing on his bandaged foot by lamp light.

"It's kinda a whodunit," he answers evasively. "Just something to pass the time."

"At least you have your book," the nurse says. "We don't have much of a lending library here."

"It's actually sorta a good story, bit of romance, if you're into that kinda thing. Passes the time anyway," he repeats, welcoming conversation.

He pulls the book from beneath the covers. "Girl stuff, really. I gave it to my sister for her birthday right before I shipped out. She's got about a dozen others. Put it in my duffle when the folks took me to the depot. Only time I seen my dad cry. Read it a coupla times already. Just looking at the pictures. Reminds me of home."

The nurse recognizes the character silhouetted in orange on the cover. She has learned never to be surprised. "Well, Private," she looks at his chart, "Novak, tell me how you managed to crush your foot." She takes a seat on the cot temporarily empty next to his.

"A piano fell on it, if you can believe it," Novak laughs. "It fell off a truck."

The nurse grins and looks at his young face for the first time. "Back home, it means you stole it when you say something fell off a truck."

"How 'bout that, where I come from too," Novak says, his breath hanging in the air from the cold.

"Where's that?" she asks.

"You wouldn't believe me if I told ya. Goose Town, we call it," he answers smiling.

"Never heard of it. But I think maybe I heard someone playing your fallen piano last night." The nurse reflects for a moment, "'Two Cigarettes in the Dark.' Unless there's even a remote chance there's more than one piano around these parts," she says looking around the low-ceilinged tent.

"Doubtful," he laughs. "Though I heard they sometimes drop two in case one didn't survive gravity." After a few seconds he chances, "Hey, what say me and you go listen to that piano tonight. I'd take you dancin' but, this foot."

She continues her examination of his foot.

"Or maybe we can catch a show at the Orpheum," Novak jokes.

"You wouldn't be the first G.I. to ask me on a date this evening," the nurse says. "Probably the youngest though."

"I'm not such a kid," Novak defends.

"No, I suppose not," the nurse replies, thinking but not saying that they all seem so young.

She turns to go but he speaks suddenly, not ready to be alone.

"Wait til they hear about the cobbler who got hobbled by a piano when I get back home."

"So you make shoes when you're not fighting for Uncle Sam?" she asks.

"Yep, 'prenticing with my dad. Novak and Son. 'A course, it's mostly mendin. Cardboard soles only last so long 'a fore you got to get new soles."

"Well, Private Novak, I think you better get a good night's rest. I imagine they'll be shipping you back up front tomorrow, bum foot and all."

"A.J," he answers.

"A. J." she repeats.

"Sure you're not up to that date?" he persists in jest. "I might not be able to find flowers this time a year, but I promise to be a perfect gentleman." Perpetuating a dream they both know has zero chance in the middle of the winter in the middle of the forest in the middle of the battle in the middle of the war, he adds, "Pick you up at six?"

"Sure," she answers, playing along. "Well, go listen to that piano and sing along."

"Jeepers Creepers, where'd you get those peepers," he sings a line.

She laughs.

"What's your name, if you don't mind my askin?" A.J. asks.

"Glynis," she answers, surprising herself. She's usually tight-lipped with personal details.

"That name's about as pretty as you are," he answers, offering her his hand. "Alexander Jakob Novak, at your service," he mimics a bow the best he can from his prone position.

At nearly 40, she knows she's far too old to be blushing at his schoolboy flirtation. She touches the crucifix hanging at her neck.

A rumble of machinery approaches the hospital tent. A rush of cold air hits them as the tent flap is opened and another nurse ducks her head in. "Captain," a woman's voice calls the nurse, Glynis, away into the night.

By light of day, Private Novak is discharged, deemed fit for duty despite his injury. Before he leaves, he asks for a pencil. The morning nurse sees him writing something but later fears he has left his book behind by mistake. Seeing the scribbled inscription in pencil, she makes up the cot for the next occupant and leaves the book on the makeshift bedside table for her captain.

## VIGNETTE THREE

## FEBRUARY 29

## "Happy Birthday"

On Mrs. Y's 100th birthday, a handful of friends, distant family, and former student cum assisted living staff made plans to assemble in the community room of her residential facility—at one time called a rest home, odious name—as a surprise to wish the old gal a happy birthday. Her husband, a jeweler in their small town, a man they remembered having a funny accent, had passed away years earlier, as had their only daughter and a grandson. So it was left to a trio of shirt tail nieces and a nephew to plan a party in their absence. In attendance were a smattering of fellow residents, a cadre of caretakers employed by the facility who happened to be representatives from various graduating classes from the nineteen fifties, sixties, seventies, and even eighties of the local high school. A great granddaughter was away at college, and no one really expected much of her anyway. A great grandson, the girl's cousin, either not be found or could not be bothered, no one was quite sure.

Oddly enough, even blood relatives in attendance thought of and referred to their aged great aunt as "Mrs. Y" more than they did something more sentimental such as "Auntie Nelle." Helen was, in actual fact, her Christian name, but few called her that, perhaps only Mr. Y. But like so many things, even that was speculative. Those inclined to think about these matters imagined that even in their home, the two called one another Mrs. and Mr. Y, respectively, Mr. Y. with his funny pronunciation. So, like everyone else for generations, even her kin had known her as Mrs. Y, the librarian at their school.

Mrs. Y assisted them with their term papers and was a wizard at helping locate microfiche articles to use as sources. She would never do the work for them, absolutely not, but she would guide them into the labyrinth of the nearby small college library on an annual research field trip day. Nowadays, students expect much more stimulating experiences if they are to board a bus with teachers for a day out of school.

Armed with rolls of dimes for reverse image xerox copies, notecards, pencils, erasers, binders, and a sack lunch, students in Comp. IV, as it was called, would hand Mrs. Y their signed permission slip and climb aboard the bus. Saying hey to Sammy, the bus driver, the sixteen or so seventeen-year-olds would take their assigned seat and ride the twelve miles to the academic library. Each had a topic that their teacher, a man with a straight part and defined comb lines, had approved. Known for always wearing a bowtie and having been a barber, and a singing one at that, during his Army days, Mr. Simpson may have made the assignment, but make no mistake, Mrs. Y was in charge of leading the expedition. Though it was well known Mr. Simpson had attended teacher training following his stint in the service on the G.I. Bill, students assumed she was somehow above Mr. Simpson in the educational chain of command.

These research pilgrimages had been going on in February since the beginning of time, as far as everyone knew. Their parents and older siblings had taken part in this rite of passage to find resources, nine at minimum drawn from books and scholarly journals, for their mid-winter Comp. IV term paper. Twelve pages, typed, double-spaced, with MLA footnotes at the bottom of each page, the papers were kept forever in whatever passed for a memory box or hope chest.

Sometimes these papers were known to resurface a year or so later at a junior college, retyped so as to erase all of the red marks, but not before making the necessary changes indicated in scarlet ink. No one thought to trade or sell their research paper, because they knew they would be found out. Furthermore, plagiarism of any kind was known to be a mortal sin, the one that would go on your permanent record and damn you for all eternity. Stories circulated of some hapless lad who had a promising baseball scholarship on the line only to have his athletic career cut short, tainted as he was with the whiff of plagiarism. Legend had it he left town in disgrace and opened a beer joint; all hopes for a chance in the Majors evaporating like so much beer foam.

Those who followed the assignment directives of Mr. Simpson, with Mrs. Y's assistance, were assured they would be successful in later life. They dutifully wrote bibliography cards for each of their sources, filled out the requisite number of quote, paraphrase, and summary note cards, made an outline complete with parallel entries for each topic, subtopic, and so on, so were certain to be in right standing to draft a paper that would need minimal revision. Of this, they were assured by the venerable librarian. The process guaranteed the product, Mrs. Y asserted annually to a new crop of industrious writers. Students suspected Mr. Simpson could be replaced in the scheme of things, and in point of fact, was when the tenor died one year over Thanksgiving break at a barbershop quartet convention after the foursome's rendition of "Easy Street."

So, on Wednesday at 1:00, those gathered in the community room festooned with colorful balloons to foist their felicitations to the town's newest centenarian, were surprised to see Mrs. Y wheeled into a chorus of "Happy Birthday!" flanked by not one, but both of her absentee great grandchildren. One of the great nieces providing accompaniment on the upright piano, hit a wrong key and stopped playing entirely.

Most of the onlookers were known to one another save one young man with unruly hair and a tablet. He approached the elderly lady and extended his hand, "I'm so happy to finally meet you in person, Mrs. Yves," he said. Raising her hand from its resting place atop the leather satchel of sorts on her lap, she said, "I'm delighted to make your acquaintance, Mr. Simpson."

"Please, call me Blake," he said.

"And you may call me Nelle. You look just like your great grandfather," the spry lady said. "He'd have something to say about your hair though."

"You know, I never met him," Blake laughed, noting her smiling eyes. "I understand you have another name that you are better known by."

"That was a long, long time ago," she said.

"I'm just sorry I couldn't meet your husband. He's equally legendary, I understand. I can't wait to hear and see more," he said, nodding at the satchel. "Shall we?" he asked, gesturing toward a table set with colorful napkins and a Tupperware container of cupcakes. The great grands set the festive confections aside.

Party throwers and partygoers stood in confused silence during this exchange between their guest of honor and the young interlopers. The smiling great granddaughter pushed her gran's chair to the table, where the great grandson gently took the satchel and placed it in front of her on the table.

The young man, Blake, opened his tablet, swiped, and flipped open a few apps before seemingly beginning to speak into the device to say, "We're here today, on February 29th to visit with one of America's longest living World War II spies, code name Hélène of Troy, on what is actually only her 25th birthday."

## VOICE THREE

## FEBRUARY 29, 1940, PARIS

### "Over the Rainbow"

Wearing a scarf and dark glasses does little to disguise the distinctive height of the woman now stepping past Claude's table. Training his eyes on her, he over fills the glass of wine from a glass decanter, nearly sloshing it on the red and white checked cloth and sets the flask on the tiny round table. He takes the menu, with a handwritten placard inserted to highlight the Jeudi special, from the couple seated before him and uses it to brush away a fly. In so doing, he bumps the back of the empty chair behind him, a lightweight folding affair, on the sidewalk tightly packed with midday diners.

He apologizes profusely to the lady whose tea was unaffected as she holds it aloft with one hand, while trying to minimize his damage with the other. He stoops to set the chair upright. Placing the menu on the table, he squares a book and saucer before her, and désolés once more to the surrounding tables lining the sidewalk. Patrons take in this clumsy spectacle, some offended, some amused, but no one unduly inconvenienced.

He cranes his neck to see that the passing tall woman has grown smaller with each passing step. In the time it takes him to remove the white apron, stuff it in a rucksack, leaving the seated cafe patrons to wonder what happened to their hapless waiter and if their déjeuner will ever arrive, the stately woman is gone. And so is the waiter. Little matter. The microfilm is safely in his apron.

Stifling her amusement to the stir caused by her leggy roommate passing by on the opposite side of the street, the lady drinking tea picks up the menu left by the waiter during his charade. She removes the daily insert, noting Bœuf Bourguignon, and tucks it in her book. She hastens back to the library to await the appointed time to proceed to the location indicated on the verso of the daily special.

To Nelle's surprise the waiter is waiting for her, or for someone anyway. This is the third time their paths have crossed, unusual in that every attempt is made to minimize repeated interaction. Personnel being in short supply, handlers realize the risk inherent in assets being seen together. Only days earlier, she had made him outside the library. Now flanked by others doing the same, he is painting a scene by the Pont Neuf. His well used watercolor set has only traces of pigment in their wells. She approaches to admire his work, not of the river before him, as the other artists are depicting but of a vase of cornflowers. She wonders if he had rather been expecting her towering auburn-tressed flat mate.

She watches him paint for a while and offers a few francs. He nods to accept her price as he untacks the still wet painting in hues of blue. He takes note of the beef bourguignon placard sticking out of the book she is carrying. He passes her the painted flowers but refuses the money. There is something familiar and quite endearing in the smile of the woman now before him. A certain liveliness in her eyes belies a subdued smile.

He closes the watercolor tin and hands it to Nelle as well. She accepts both the painting and the tin. She has been instructed to take the contents from the paint set to her next drop the following day. There she will hand off four small diamonds, this time in a box of matches. She cannot be certain, but she imagines they will somehow be used in service of the Resistance. Usually, her role has been confined to surreptitious transfer of undeveloped film of open source documents in the form of propaganda books and foreign newspapers, passed along to better know the enemy. Her efficiency has garnered her greater responsibilities and even a codename, unbeknownst to her.

The cornflower painting she keeps, privately fancying it a gift for her 24th birthday, but only her sixth birthday celebrated on her birth date in actual point of fact. This is the closest to receiving flowers from a man that she has ever experienced, but she is not foolish or unprofessional enough to make anything of the gesture, especially in light of his convincing performance to her roommate's appearance.

Their recruitment by "Wild Bill" Donovan himself upon the recommendation of Librarian of Congress Archibald MacLeish for whom they both worked in Washington has placed Nelle and Velma, the taller of the two, working in the field for which they had been trained, that of information services as part of the Interdepartmental Committee for the Acquisition of Foreign Publications (IDC). One a country girl from Kansas and the other a sophisticate from Connecticut, the two assigned to the Office of Strategic Services are billeted together because no one takes particular notice of the after-hours activities of two librarians. As they work opposite shifts, Nelle, overseeing the archives overnight, leaves each morning as Velma arrives to work the reference desk by day. They are rarely seen together. It's unusual for her not to be sleeping on a weekday, but she had marked off the night before, ostensibly for her birthday rather than for a clandestine mission.

The skills of the hapless waiter, Claude, are not limited to painting pretty pictures of flowers. Fluent in English, German, and French, the Luxembourg-born expat has participated in both world wars, currently most useful to the Allies for his expertise as a gemologist. His privileged upbringing has provided him with musical training, in addition to an apprenticeship to a lapidary, both skills surprisingly useful in his line of espionage. The lingering effects of exposure to mustard gas in the first world war has left his health unsuited to traditional military service when it proved not to be the war to end all wars.

The scenario in spycraft at the cafe falls on the heels of intelligence that someone called Hélène of Troy from the bibliothèque would be contacting him. Having watched the comings and goings for a full week at the library's opening and closing times, he has registered a statuesque beauty. Seeing her pass by the cafe earlier had thrown him for a loop. He had taken little note of the woman who had been watching him days earlier and situated herself at the ready in the cafe to make the drop. As she walks away with watercolor tin and the cornflower painting he had anticipated giving to someone else, Claude marvels that perhaps this woman is the one they call Hélène of Troy. Naturally, he has never heard of Kansas, much less of Troy, her hometown.

Months later Claude finds himself miles away on another mission, this time of a musical nature, when he is asked to tune a recently arrived sturdy green piano that would be used to entertain troops in a U.S.O show. Although not trained for tuning exactly, he begins with C and adjusts string tension and set pins until the Victory Vertical Steinway is passably in tune.

He stays to play the sheet music that came packed along with tuning tools. In an impromptu concert, he works his way through the anthology of American patriotic and show tunes, more familiar to those who gather to listen and sing, than to him. One song they all know is "Over the Rainbow." For his final number, he taps out the never-before-played notes of a waltz that has been going through his head for some time. The elegant rise-and-fall action with a 1-2-3 rhythm in lovely 3/4 time flows from his fingers as he imagines dancing with a librarian, the shorter of two and the one with smiling eyes, whose fleeting acquaintance he made in Paris. He thinks he will call this composition "Hélène."

\*\*\*\*\*\*\*\*\*\*

*Librarianship and spy craft are well-suited partners; both revolve around the collection and dissemination of information. Librarians understand that information possession is not enough. It requires organization and analysis to make such information meaningful. World War II catalysed vital shifts in the world of library sciences, from a greater recognition of the role of women, to the embrace of new technologies, to increased government reliance on research institutions. Cooperation is key when it comes to winning a war. Information has a crucial role in that equation.*

Ivry, Sara. "How American Librarians Helped Defeat the Nazis."*JSTOR Daily*, 29 Nov. 2023, **https://daily.jstor.org**/how-american-librarians -helped-defeat-the-nazis/.

## VIGNETTE FOUR

## MARCH

### "Fur Elise"

"Hey stranger," the woman said, accepting his kiss on the cheek and welcoming the man inside her house. The man followed the older woman through the living room to the kitchen.

Frank leaned against his aunt's counter as she took two Mickey Mouse glasses from a cabinet. "I wanted to come see you before now but you're always gallivanting around the country. Where were you over the winter?" Frank asked the woman. Her athletic apparel gave a youthful appearance despite her age and having let her black hair go white.

"Fredericksburg," Mildred said, as she poured a splash of Bacardi into two glasses filled with diet Coke and ice. "Texas," she added for clarification.

"What on earth do you do when you're down there?" Frank asked, genuinely curious what his widowed aunt, not so distant in age from him but his only living older relative, did with her time.

"There's so much to do and only a few months to get it all in. Used to go to Corpus Christi but one can only walk along the beach so much. Play pickleball, cards, garden," she added more to the point.

Frank couldn't imagine playing anything with pickles, but he loved Texas Hold 'Em. Still, he doubted he would enjoy being away from home and Paige and Molly for so long. "Any Longhorn suitors?" Frank joked.

"Very funny. A few contenders, clumsy old codgers," she said smiling. "Most of the people in my retirement community are from up North. Mind if we take these to the porch?" she asked, handing him a drink.

If it were up to him, he would have been happy to sit in the kitchen, but his mom's younger brother's wife wasn't one to stay indoors if she could be outside.

The two sat on a porch swing in the brisk spring air, the first mild day of March. Frank looked at his watch.

"Days are finally getting longer," he remarked.

"Thank goodness. I see some crocuses popping up," she nodded toward the yard. "I didn't have a chance to clean out the flowerbeds before I went South."

"Pauline always took care of that," Frank mused, thinking of his own untended lawn.

"So, what brings you around?" his aunt Milly asked, taking a sip.

"I found something and couldn't think of anyone else who might be able to shed any light on it," Frank said, reaching inside his jacket pocket. He handed a small, folded sheet of paper with praying hands on the cover to the older woman.

"What's this?" Milly asked.

"Not sure. I thought maybe you could tell me," he answered.

"Let me look," Milly said, setting her rum and diet Coke on the porch and drying her hands on her Adidas leggings before taking the program. She was silent for several seconds. "Be right back." Then she stood and dashed back into the house. Several minutes later she returned with a small, lacquered box in her hands. She handed it to Frank. He lifted the lid and a few faint but familiar bars of music played, enough for Frank to recognize but not identify the melody of "Fur Elise." The tune faded out entirely.

"I was thinking about this awhile back. How long have you had it?" Frank asked, turning the shiny box over.

"Since Ginny gave it to my mom. Maybe 60 years." Frank wound the key and, reanimated, the little comb and cylinder came to life, played as if by unseen tiny hands. Frank inspected the plush green interior, as well as the contents of the box.

"Go ahead," his aunt encouraged.

He moved a crucifix necklace to the side with a finger and drew a folded strip of heavy paper from the velvet lining. Unfolding it, he looked at four one-inch square black and white pictures stacked together vertically. He looked at the two couples crammed into the frame, forever youthful.

"That one girl looks a heck of a lot like Paige when she was in high school."

"With good reason. That's her grandma," Milly said.

"Well, I'll be darned," he said, looking closer. "I've seen pictures of Mom when she was young, but not like this. She was always beautiful, but I don't think I've ever seen her look so . ." he tried to come up with the right word.

"Playful?" Milly suggested.

"Yeah," Frank said, marveling at how alive she appeared looking directly at him from the past. "How much did a photo booth cost back in the day?"

"Maybe two bits. I wouldn't know. I wasn't even born. Those are my folks."

"Really? I guess I assumed that's you," he said, pointing to a woman with curly hair.

"Just how old do you think I am?" she laughed. "No, that couple are my mom and dad," Milly said, indicating the ageless couple.

"Now that I look at it, I can see you in the man's face," Frank conceded. "The eyes, I think. I never knew your folks."

"Well, I didn't even know my dad much except through letters. They say I got his jet-black hair and green eyes. Not that you can tell by the picture. Or by me these days!" she laughed, pointing to her snowy white hair.

"You still have the sparkly green eyes though," Frank offered.

"He was gone by the time I was even school age," Milly said. "Funny how you can miss someone you don't really even remember," she reflected. "There's a void to this day."

Changing her tone, she took the photo strip from Frank. "Dad was visiting Mom from back East where he grew up. Met her when she won a baking contest and went by train on a trip to New York. It was in all the papers, how a hometown girl won a contest for her coconut cream pie recipe, and they sent her to the Big Apple!"

Frank laughed and pointed at the man with his arm around his mom. "Pop sure had a full head of hair back then."

"Oh," Milly said. "That's not your dad."

Frank's eyebrows raised in surprise. "What?" He took a pair of readers from his shirt pocket and held the photo away from him for closer inspection. "Then who is he?"

Milly reached for the music box and drew out the only other thing inside. She handed it to Frank. It was a folded program with praying hands on the cover, identical to the one Frank had brought. "That's the fella your mom was engaged to marry."

Frank sat in stunned silence. "I had no idea," he finally said.

"Crazy to think that both men would be drafted, shipped off to serve in the Pacific," she said, "and never return."

"The ultimate sacrifice," Frank murmured, knowing only that Sergeant Eastman had died at Luzon and having heard that Aunt Milly's father had been declared missing in action, feared POW, in the war.

The two finished their drinks quietly, and Frank stood to leave. "Don't be a stranger," Aunt Milly said.


## VOICE FOUR

## AN ISLAND IN THE PACIFIC THEATER, MARCH 1942

### "Don't Fence Me In"

### "Boogie Woogie Bugle Boy of Company B"


As the timid ensign limps to the end of "When the Saints Go Marching In" on the sturdy blue-gray piano, Michael takes a seat at the end of the flight deck bench just as the ecumenical service draws to a close. A chaplain steps to the podium and says, "Please will you bow with me in prayer." It's phrased as a request but meant as a direct order.

"What happened to your face, Paddy?" the seaman from the arid desert of the Texas panhandle asks out of the side of his mouth.

"He was born that way," his sidekick from the other side of the Lone Star State sing songs, "Weren't you, Yankee Doodle?"

"He's a dandy, awlright" the first Texan drawls.

"You yahoos got a problem with the lad, you take it up with me," the aviator sitting behind them growls, the black top of his bowed crew cut visible out of their peripheral vision. "Amen," he says brightly as the prayer comes to an end, crossing himself. Michael crosses himself as well, feeling secure in so doing without all the usual Irish Catholic commentary for once.

The shipboard makeshift congregants disband behind the two skedaddling sailors, and the pilot extends his hand. "Cahill."

Michael looks at both of his gauze-wrapped mits, and then offers his bandaged right hand. "Captain," he replies, nodding. "Ah, Boyle, Michael," he adds by way of introduction, trying not to wince as they shook. Cahill looks away from the plasters covering Boyle's face.

"Thanks for fixing up 'Empire State Enchantress,'" Cahill says, segueing from Boyle's patched face to account for his defense of the lanky injured mechanic earlier.

Michael searches his memory bank for visual images of nose art on recent planes he's worked on during this most recent spate of island hopping and lands on one he recognizes. A buxom woman clutching the Empire State Building. "On Tinian," he says, remembering the island. "Superfortress," he adds. "She'd taken some flak."

"She sure did," Cahill laughs. "And I had to get a new pair of britches." The two fall in behind those heading toward the gangplank, one tall, skinny, and banged up, the other a clean-cut poster boy Naval Academy cadet. The captain nods toward the direction of the two mouthy but quickly departed crew members ahead of them as they wind through the squadron milling around on deck.

"So did you, take some flak, I mean," Cahill says.

"Oh, those bumpkins, Billings and Byers. Last two islands, we were in the same hut. They're dumb but mostly harmless. My mom always asks why all my buddies have last names that begin with B when I write home. Outta 26 letters, sometimes wish I'd not been born a B. Or better, they were Williams or Zuckermans. Looks like we're stuck together by virtue of our last names for the duration of the war."

"Know what you mean. The military does like the alphabet. I'm always writing my wife and daughter about Cabot, Carneal, and Collins." Remembering Boyle's harassers, Cahill says, "Actually, I was talking your face. That's a lot of scrapes. What happened to you? And to your hands for that matter?"

"Showing off. Jumped off a Seabee's doodlebug and tried to do a handstand on the beach. I can walk on my hands for hours back on Coney Island, but I didn't take the coral on these beaches into account. Not as forgiving as sand." Boyle shakes his head at his own stupidity. "I didn't tell any of that to the medic. He musta picked a dozen shells out of my right hand alone," Boyle adds, holding up his swaddled paw.

The two pass the starboard Vertical Victory Steinway that blends in with the battleship color pallet. "There goes your chance for ever playing Carnegie Hall," Cahill jokes.

"Close call," Boyle agrees. "I was hopeless on the piano anyway. You related to a jarhead named Cahill I met on Okinawa?"

"No, got a brother in the Army Air Corp though. Italy, last I knew."

"Just wondered. Got a lotta respect for the Marines, 'specially the ones that took Tinian." Boyle remembers how they secured the island to make way for an amphibious landing.

The two reach the end of the gangplank and turn to go in different directions, but not before Cahill picks up a couple of coconuts lying on the ground. "Wife makes the world's best coconut pie," he says, tossing one to Michael. "Hey, it's been good to meet you, Boyle. We

Bronx Bombers gotta stick together." Cahill slaps the mechanic on the back.

No time to eat before reporting in at 13:00, Boyle walks the few miles from the rugged coast toward a clearing with a series of Quonset repair shops and hangars deeper in the jungle. He sips from the coconut he'd had one heck of a time cracking open to drink.

Thoughts of his dad and mom come unbidden, and he tries to distract himself from homesickness by thinking about anything other than home. His mind lands on the humorous bureaucratic incompetence that led him to the South Seas. He recalls how when he was first called up, he traveled from New York to California, only to find the Navy didn't have his paperwork so they sent him back to NYC by train. There he was sent right back to California, this time with a stop in Kansas City at Union Station.

He remembered listening to a swing band right there in the depot and dancing to "Don't Sit Under the Apple Tree" with a brunette named Patricia who had sold him a pack of cigarettes. Just the memory of the whistle of the trains coming into the station makes him homesick all over as they call to mind the sound of the elevated trains going through Brooklyn. Before leaving on Uncle Sam's dime to come 8,500 miles from home, the farthest he'd ever been was a summer camp for boys in the Catskills. He'd been homesick then too and had added salty tears to the mildewy pillow in his cabin. He hated to cry, had thought it unmanly, until his dad had taken him to the train station to see him off for the first time. There they had both wept. Boyle mainly because he had never seen his old man cry. His dad, a veteran of the War to End all Wars, was the most stoic guy he'd ever met.

Still thinking of home when he reaches the airfield, Boyle dons his grease-stained coveralls. He'd had a helluva time with the buttons. He's not entirely sure how well he'll be able to turn a wrench with his hands wrapped as they are. He looks at the bulletin board for his Sunday assignment. Tacked to the board is an insignia of Mickey Mouse straddling a torpedo, both gloved hands gripping twin blazing machine guns. "Feel for ya, Buddy," Boyle says to Walt's little morale boosting cartoon friend.

He notes the flight mission itinerary thumbtacked above the mechanic's list. Toward the top, he notes Cabot, Cahill, Carneal, and Collins, and their destination, Solomon Islands.

Two weeks later Boyle is on the same ship having a drink with Billings and Byers, waiting for a U.S.O. show to begin. His hands have pretty much healed, but a white piece of medical tape reminds the barrack bumpkins of Boyle's earlier coral encounter. They don't say a word, recalling Cahill's threats. Today they are teasing him about his Noo Yawk accent. "You're just jealous 'cause you aren't from a place so nice they named it twice," Boyle says, defending his hometown. The show begins. "And at least I'm not from Hoop and Holler," he shouts to Byers, as music begins to play.

The master of ceremonies says, "Give it up for Harry, our first act!" To tepid applause at the introduction, the entertainer born Harry Lillis Crosby leaps on stage and the crowd's enthusiasm grows tenfold. Bing begins singing, "Oh, give me land, lots of land under starry skies above, Don't fence me in. Let me ride through the wide-open country that I love. Don't fence me in" to the delight of Byers and Billings, who sing along, most unfortunately, at the top of their lungs.

Boyle leaves the two Lone Star lugs to bellow their twangy duet and steps out of their range to better hear the crooner's song. He looks over the water, the smoke of his cigarette obscuring the view. Midway through the Cole Porter tune, and to much whooping and hollering, the Andrew Sisters take the stage to finish out the song with Crosby before launching into their signature "Boogie Woogie Bugle Boy of Company B."

Bing sits in for the drummer on the next number, and the trio sister act stays on to sing "Rum and Coca-Cola" to a Calypso beat. "Working for the Yankee dollar," they harmonize to the accompaniment of an animated midshipman on a familiar blue-gray piano. Where once a timid ensign wanly welcomed the Saints marching in during the topside Sunday service a fortnight ago, Boyle had met the dark-haired captain. According to the amended posting on the billboard, Cahill never returned from his mission to the Solomon Islands. Boyle figures he might try to look up some Cahills if he ever makes it back home to the old neighborhood.

**VIGNETTE FIVE**

**APRIL**

**"Moonlight Serenade"**

The ordinarily loquacious and rambunctious sixth graders, clad in the red, white, and black plaid of their school dress code, filed into the empty classroom with uncharacteristic silence. Each took a seat without having to be told, much to the delight of their teacher who, in all fairness, had instructed them beforehand to do exactly that. Still, she felt pride in their respectful demeanor and marveled that they were, in fact, capable of listening and following instructions. All it took apparently was to have a 95-year-old visitor seated at the front of the room.

Even despite having just finished a novel about siblings during World War II who were evacuated from their home in London to the countryside, the twenty 12-year-olds could scarcely appreciate the immense emotional toil it must have taken on families to be separated in this manner. The nonagenarian before them now was about to enlighten them, having lived through the experience as a young girl the age of her great granddaughter. Unlike the infants and toddlers who made up the majority of those billeted with families in the countryside, Charlotte Burns had been their age, an adolescent, sent with two younger sisters and a brother to escape the nightly bombing raids over England's skies. Decades later and in the heartland of America, the elderly woman still carried vestiges of otherness in her speech and in her bearing. "Good morning," she greeted the children with false bravado and a life-long accent.

Charlotte Burns had never been comfortable speaking before gatherings of any size, and the prospect of addressing a roomful of upper elementary students filled her with terror. She had agreed because her great granddaughter had asked her to speak to her classmates, and Charlotte would do anything for Charlie. So when Charlie's teacher contacted her on behalf of the class, Mrs. Burns agreed. She had even gone to the beauty shop to have her hair set and worn her nicest outfit, red, white, and blue for her native and for her adopted homeland.

Following a brief introduction, for the children knew that they were to have a guest speaker who was related to their friend Charlie, the teacher, Miss Jackson, gave Charlotte Burns the floor and asked her for some general background on what it was like living in England during the war.

For a time, the woman sat in silence, looking over the heads of the students seated before her. During this uncomfortable duration, the students remained quiet but looked around at one another with only minimal head movement. Only Charlie kept her brown eyes trained on Gran, as she called her. She smiled at her great grandmother and gave a slight nod of reassurance, though the woman appeared not to see or register this intended encouragement.

"The buzz bombs were quite frightening," the woman finally said, faintly enough the children strained to hear. "I can still hear them to this day," she reflected, seeming to indeed hear the characteristic buzz of the low altitude, cross-shaped flying bombs. "When their timing mechanisms went off, they would fall to earth and explode. We knew when the buzzing stopped, we had to take cover right away."

Mrs. Burns stopped at that point, to recollect and collect her next thoughts before speaking. "I was about your age. I remember Mr. Chamberlain came on the wireless when Germany invaded Poland. That was 1939. After the attack on Pearl Harbor, the Americans joined the war, finally." As she voiced her thoughts, which came in no particular order, her voice and her confidence grew stronger.

"The air raids had us dashing to the Anderson at all hours," she said of the backyard shelter her father buried as a protective fortress for the family. "It was our subterranean garden," she laughed. "We had to take our gas masks with us everywhere, even to school. I hated them. But the Germans had used the mustard gas in the last war so there were fears Mr. Hitler might too."

Miss Jackson was thankful the novel the class had read aloud had made mention of many of the fragmented thoughts that Mrs. Burns alluded to. She did not wish to interrupt their guest with questions or explanations, but Mrs. Jackson took mental note of items that might require clarification for her students, each of whose own grandparents were born long after the war. Charlie was an anomaly, having been born to successive generations of older parents. With each detail, Charlie would smile and bob her head, having heard few of the details that seemed to emerge from Gran after decades of dormancy.

"We would count the RAF planes as they flew out over the Channel and then count them again when they returned. They always flew out right over the treetops, wave after wave in groupings of three," she said. "We always hoped for an equal number on the return flight, but they came back high overhead, in pairs or often alone," she added wistfully.

Mrs. Burns smiled. "The wireless was always on. I loved it any time BBC played 'White Cliffs of Dover.' And I paid special attention when Mr. Churchill was speaking," she said of their new P.M. "I still prefer to listen to my news," she reflected, jumping forward in time.

Suddenly a series of stray thoughts came to Mrs. Burns, and she looked directly at Charlie. "When we went to live in Yorkshire, we were rationed to one egg a week. I always gave mine to Tommy because he was such a growing boy. We ate bread and dripping on days we were lucky enough to have meat to fry. Everyone got one new suit of clothes a year. We hardly grew from one year to the next, but the old outfits did show wear. I don't remember much else about that time away from home. I've tried to forget. There were the four of us. We stayed with a vicar and his wife. I just tried to keep us together under one roof and counted the days until we could return home."

Her stream of consciousness took a detour to the danger surrounding her father's driving at night under blackout conditions. "He was an electrician and had to work seven days a week as well as serve on a volunteer fire brigade called out to battle fires caused by incendiaries."

Mrs. Burns said that her dad didn't begrudge his service because others had sacrificed so much more. His nephew Nigel, who was in the Royal Marines. was captured and held on Crete. "He escaped three times before he was shot and killed," she added, almost matter-of-factly.

The students leaned forward with rapt attention at this unexpected revelation. Just as quickly, Mrs. Burns moved on to a different topic.

"Everything was rationed, sugar, tea, cheese. Mum had to stand in line for cuts of meat. I don't imagine you lot have had to eat much heart or tripe," she said, her eyes twinkling as she connected with those of her audience. Not a single student had ever even heard of tripe, but the mere thought of eating heart evoked exaggerated squirming and polite grimacing.

"I brought along this ration book to show you. I've kept it all these years." Mrs. Burns reached into her white sweater pocket for a small tan booklet that Charlie jumped up to take and pass among her friends. The complicated little journal was dated and stamped to log the allotted items for each family by the Ministry of Food. As the booklet passed from one to the next, students noted the limited and basic nature of grocery items. Pizza, tacos, and chicken nuggets were nowhere listed, which seemed to solidify the children's youthful admiration for the older woman's endured privations.

Those deprivations during her youth visibly strengthened their respect for Mrs. Burns and reinforced her resolve to impart something meaningful to this generation. She in no way begrudged their lack of want and privileges. Their life experiences were so very different from hers, and perhaps even more difficult in some ways, but 12-year-olds are much the same all over the world.

Mrs. Burns looked at the students one by one for a time, seeming to take in their uniformed appearance for the first time. She reached Charlie and their eyes, hers a pale blue, and her great granddaughter's dark with flecks of amber, sparked in recognition. Mrs. Burns shook her head and smiled. "I could never make my mum happy," she confessed. "Any time I wore an outfit that met with her disapproval, she would threaten, 'You never know when you might meet the Queen.'" This she said in a tremulous voice as if to mimic her mum.

"Did you ever meet her, the Queen?" a girl in the back blurted.

"No dear. I saw her once and waved. I've taken up so much of your time," Mrs. Burns said, turning to the teacher.

"Perhaps we have time for one or two more questions," the teacher countered.

"Gran, what was it like when you and your sisters and brothers had to go live in the country, away from your family?" her granddaughter asked.

"We just got on with it," her great grandmother stated dismissively, awaiting the next question.

"What kind of music do you like?" a boy nearly shouted, provoking laughter from his peers.

"Oh, I enjoy all types of music. When I was your age I was particularly fond of your Glenn Miller, 'Moonlight Serenade.'" The boy showed no signs of knowing why she referred to anyone as his Glenn Miller. "In later years, I grew to love jazz."

"What movies did you like?" a girl next to Charlie asked.

"I loved the pictures as a girl, especially anything with Vivian Leigh. She's English, you know. I was quite taken with *Gone with The Wind*. The first film I saw in colour at the cinema in our neighborhood. I quite fancied Clark Gable."

Miss Jackson heard Charlie whisper something in a feigned Southern accent to her astonished friend, who clutched her hands to her mouth to stifle her laughter.

"Mrs. Burns, how did you come to live in the U.S?" Mrs. Jackson inquired abruptly.

Checking the time on the watch hanging from a short fob pinned upside down to her sweater, Mrs. Burns fast-forwarded a few years. "Well, it wasn't until the early 1970's. After the war I trained in midwifery in London," she sighed. "That's where I met Mr. Burns. Outside a lying-in hospital near the Covent Garden Tube station. My Archie was a G.I. from the States stationed in the United Kingdom. Until I met him, I had never known a black person."

## VOICE FIVE

## RURAL ENGLAND, 1943

### "Jumpin at the Woodside"

*"Pay attention men, we're about to toss you a ball—it's Jubilee. Step on your footlockers, men, and hang on to your hats. We're gettin' groovy as a 10-cent movie. You've been listening to the sounds of the feminine portion of the broadcast with Thelma Carpenter. Before that we heard Jimmie "Five by Five" Rushing. Buddy Wilson, no relation, and his sensational aggregation of jazz gyration kicked open our show by extending greetings to the gang at MotorTorpedo Squadron 2 and the HQ CO Willys-Overland mechanics at APO 508 and their original composition, "B-Flat Bebop" I'm your master of ceremonies, Dooley Wilson.*

*"Let's welcome our next guest. He is no newcomer to the show but lotsa fellas have written lotsa letters, askin' us to put you and the boys back on the beam. So here to remind you he's still tops in our hot scat jump parade with a hunk of hot that'll bounce you right out of your quonset hut is "Jumpin at the Woodside" by the one and only Count Basie and his orchestra on Armed Forces Radio Service."*

"Hear that? I am on the radio! Or as good as," T/5 Archibald Burns says, snapping off the garage tuner and picking up a well-worn wooden bat.

"He didn't say your name, fool. Not any more than he said my name or Davis or Sanders," Ike Washington argues, lacing his boots.

"The man said 'the Willys-Overland mechanics at APO 508,'" Burns reminds him. "Last I checked that be us."

"We fixed the man's Jeep. Got him to his next gig, s'all. And now he's all the way in Californ-i-a," Davis says, tossing the baseball against the wall and catching it bare-handed.

"He said he'd give us a shout out," Burns adds.

"I can't believe someone we played a set with was on Jubilee radio," Sanders says, fingers riff riding in the air.

"Good thing you can dance the ivories, 'cause you sho can't dance," Burns says.

"'Course we had to wait til those white cats got off th' stage," Washington mumbles. "All worth it when Sandy made that ugly ol' piano sing," Burns says.

"May been ugly, but closest thing to a Steinway I'll ever play," Sanders reasons.

Suddenly Major Heckman is standing in the doorway. "Come on guys, we got a game to play."

"Yessir!" Davis says for the men as all snap to attention. As the major retreats, Davis stuffs the ball under his armpit and claps his hands. "Play ball."

"It don't mean a thing if it ain't got that swing," Burns sings, swinging his bat.

"Doo-ah, doo-ah, doo-ah," Davis choruses.

Sanders grabs a pair of cut-off cotton jersey gloves and stuffs them in the back pocket of his fatigues. Washington throws Sanders a well-worn baseball mitt. "Can't risk those tender ticklers."

The four walk to the door of the Quonset garage.

"Who's on first," Davis says.

"I don't know," the foursome replies.

"I don't know's on third," Sanders chimes.

"I don't care," says Washington.

"That's our shortstop," they chant in unison, laughing at their improv.

"You guys are a gas," Burns says of their riff on Abbott and Costello and puts out the lights.

Each of the four grabs a khaki jacket with the words 'Heckman's Hepcats' inked across the back from a hook. They join a half a dozen other players walking toward the vacant cricket pitch in the village.

There the musical mechanics and the rest of their crew meet up with Spade's Aces, a rival team from the 151st Quartermaster Truck Regiment, under the command of Major Morlock Spader for a Lancashire sandlot showdown of the ages. Bamber Bridge townsfolk used to lengthy cricket matches pack the stands, fortified with sausage rolls and thermoses of tea. The game is a delight on many levels, not the least for the novelty of America's favorite pastime. Seeing so many black faces engaged in friendly competition is also a curiosity for the Anglo-Saxon descendants.

With Burns at short, Davis on the mound, Sanders in center, and Washington behind the plate, the game goes 11 innings. Spectators used to interminable test matches do not find this duration exceptional. With the Hepcats on top after a walk-off home run by Washington, Sanders writes of their victory home to his brother, a reporter for the *Pittsburgh Courier*, the paper known for its Double Victory Campaign–championing Victory Abroad against fascism and Victory at Home against racial oppression.

History at large will never know about this epic encounter that featured an enlisted Negro League player on either side and a future Major League left fielder. This last thanks in no small way to the as-yet unforeseen pioneer efforts of another, a commissioned 2nd Lieutenant currently serving stateside, the one-day Dodger with #42 on his jersey.

However, a footnote in history a few months later will record another event that took place at Bamber Bridge. To those in the know, Bamber Bridge becomes a symbol of resilience and racial unity after locals sided with black officers in a confrontation with white MPs.

Still readers of the *Courier* and listeners of the AFRS Jubilee radio broadcast may have heard mention of the game's outcome from MC Dooley Wilson, later to become better known as the pianist Sam to whom Ingrid Bergman tells to play a song for old time's sake.


## VIGNETTE SIX

## MAY

## "Abide with Me"

Jo rushed into the carpeted vestibule and hastily signed the guest register. She noted that the organ was playing a familiar refrain in the sanctuary. A large jovial man in a bespoke suit whispered, "Hi Jo. It's nice to see you again. I'm so sorry about your grandmother. I'm glad you could make it. The service has just started." He reached out to take her dry raincoat and hung it on a hook and handed her a program.


Jo briefly wondered how the man knew her name. She walked where he had motioned to go, up the center aisle to the front pews. Slipping in beside her mother, Noelle, in an empty spot saved for her, Jo held out her hand for her mother to squeeze. She had arrived in time.

"I'm glad you're here, honey," Noelle said into her ear and brushed her cheek with a kiss. With a sigh, Jo's body stilled, but her mind was still racing. She told herself to calm down. The organ melody that filled the vaulted sanctuary was at once recognizable, yet its title escaped her completely.

She hadn't attended church since childhood. Even then she had gone only on the very few occasions she stayed overnight with her grandparents. They had been members of the very congregation she sat among now, alongside relatives, many of whom she hadn't seen for years.

What must they think of her, waltzing in late to her grandmother's funeral? Her flight had been delayed due to heavy storms. The crystalline sky above in her hometown had belied the torrential rainfall overnight. Wet streets were the only evidence that it had rained locally.

The phrase "fast falls the eventide" came unbidden to her thoughts in time with the music. She turned her attention back to the song. "Help of the helpless, Lord," followed by the next line. "Abide with Me." That was it. It all came back to her, and she mentally heard, hit and miss, the words to "Abide With Me" in final refrain.

As the song drew to an end, its mystery solved, Jo felt the relief of being able to concentrate on the service. She took in the flowers and the urn on a small table. She marveled that her grandmother, who was once every bit of five eleven and so full of life, could be reduced to its dusty contents. Although in her later years, Velma Martin had seemed to shrink, her personality still loomed large. Forever suggesting Jo read this book, date that boy, pursue this major, attend this college. Jo felt she had finally done something right when she followed Grandma Vel's suggestion to open a bookstore with that MBA she earned from her grandmother's alma mater in Connecticut.

A man was reading a passage of scripture, something from Psalms, but despite her best intentions, Jo wasn't following a word he was saying.

She wasn't well-versed about the Bible, but she remembered the pastor reading from *Job* 3 at her grandfather's funeral ten years earlier. She remembered this stray fact because it was the first time she had heard the book properly pronounced as *Job*, and not job, as she had imagined it. That had been a decade earlier in this very church. Only Grandpa Noel had not been cremated. A flag-draped coffin contained the empty shell his soul had vacated.

She smiled to recall how he had once told Jo when she was a little girl that he hadn't just married a librarian; he'd married a tall red-headed drink of water. "Smart and good-lookin." Noel Martin said even Uncle Sam, try as he might, couldn't keep them apart. Destined for one another, they had exchanged letters for years from different sides of the planet. Jo visualized two tiny people writing at desks on opposite longitudinal hemispheres of a globe. Velma and Noel had shared sixty years of marriage before he died.

But by the time of his death, Noel Martin had been alive but not living for years, dementia having robbed him of any recognition of who his loved ones were. Jo always found it odd that her grandma, who found a silver lining in every situation, took some measure of comfort in her husband's loss of memory. Jo recalled her having said it was a blessing that he could finally forget some things.

Jo had asked her mother how that could even be possible, for there to be anything good about losing one's memory. That was when her mother told what little she knew of the terrors Jo's grandfather had known during his time in the service. A quiet man by nature, Noel Martin had cried out in his sleep after returning from the "Pacific Operation," as she always heard her parents refer to it. Every night he relived some unimaginable horror.

Noelle's mother Velma, Jo's grandmother, didn't know, or at least had never shared with her daughter, many details, only that as a young corporal Grandpa Noel had experienced whatever it was that revisited him by night. From the mid-twentieth century to the beginning of the twenty-first, Noel Martin battled malignant spirits every night back on American soil with the resources available to those who refused to talk about it, namely faith and whiskey. Clients who knew Noel Martin as their quiet but efficient insurance agent in civilian life would never have guessed he met each new day following sleepless hours numbed with alcohol. The onset of Alzheimer's had robbed him of recognizing family members, but at least it had exorcised his demons. He spent the rest of his years in peaceful but sober oblivion.

Jo felt her mother sobbing beside her, which brought her attention back to the service at hand. Jo reached for a box of tissues under the pew, but an elderly woman behind them beat her to it and handed Noelle a Kleenex. Jo realized that like Grandma, her once statuesque mother seemed small beside her.

The large man in the sharp suit who had welcomed Jo stepped up on the podium and addressed those assembled. "Ms. Velma, ever organized, had pre-arranged every aspect of her service. From the music and the passage of scripture to the obituary and the choice of who would deliver her eulogy, Ms. Velma left nothing to chance. It is at this point in the order of service she planned herself that she asked that I read the contents of this sealed envelope. I'm supposing it is a goodbye or an elegy of sorts but all I know for sure is it is something she felt compelled to share with you upon her death. It is not anything you'll find printed in your bulletin, but rather something she penned in her own hand."

The large man settled a pair of glasses on his nose and drew an envelope from the inner pocket of his suit jacket. He took a deep breath and slit open the envelope. He unfolded the letter inside and cleared his voice. "I have not always been who you think I am," he read slowly in a big voice.

## VOICE SIX

## PACIFIC THEATER, MAY 1944

### "We'll Meet Again"

Corporal Noel Martin steps on the scale and watches as the orderly balances it and records his weight. He glances at the clipboard to see if there are still three digits in the box. There are. He must be holding his own despite not having eaten his dinner.

He shuffles back to a cot where he gingerly sits and musters the strength to swing his legs onto the thin mattress. Martin lies back and adjusts the gown open to the back to cover what's left of him. The voluminous johnny gown does so easily.

Martin sees that there are two envelopes on his tray table. He recognizes the handwriting at once, but he makes no move toward opening it or the official looking one peeking out from behind it. In seconds he is asleep.

Somewhere in his sleep he finds himself back in the thick of the jungle behind enemy lines. In this nightly episode, it is his third day on the island, but he is not hungry. So far he has found plenty to eat, foraging as trained for edible plants and small animals.

He hears people speaking at the top of their lungs in a confusing tongue. Despite not understanding their language, he knows they are shrieking orders to someone unseen. He creeps closer for a better vantage point to relay information later from a safe distance. His heart begins to race. He knows what is coming and flails his way out of exhausted slumber, hardly disturbing the convalescence of the men berthed on either side of him, plagued as they are from their own nightmares.

Staring at the ceiling in the darkness above him, Martin feels the heart jolting inside his chest slow down precipitously. Someone standing over him turns on a lamp and hands him a glass of water. He takes it and gratefully takes a sip, spilling more than he swallows. Thirsty he takes a larger gulp but chokes, the pain of aspiration almost not worth the effort of hydration. A hand in the dark gently pats his back.

"Do you want to talk about it?" the voice in white asks softly. Martin repeats the unspoken answer to the voice for the twelfth consecutive day by rolling over in reply.

He falls back into the same unconsciousness punctuated by recurring visions of G.I.s tortured at the hands of their captors. Martin's real-time screams drown out that of the Americans in his nightmare. Alerting the captors to the Marine Ranger watching from just beyond the dense forest line, they turn and advance on him.

Morning comes but Martin doesn't fully wake until nearly noon. His fitful rest leaves him lethargic despite days spent in bed. A tray of cold eggs, bacon congealed in grease, and soggy toast are on the tray next to a cold coffee. The letters are nowhere to be found. He doesn't have the energy to care. The news can't be good.

The double doors to the ward open and the sounds of a phonograph playing in the distance slip in fleetingly. The scratchy recording of Dame Vera Lynn sings, "When the lights go on again all over the world, and the boys are home again all over the world, and rain or snow is all that may fall from the skies above, A kiss won't mean goodbye, but Hello to love."

Martin has seen Vera Lynn take the stage for an impromptu duet with Bob Hope. The English chanteuse was accompanied by a pianist playing a dark green piano singing "White Cliffs of Dover" during a joint rally for American and British troops.

"For a morale boosting song, that one's a helluva gut punch," the voice in the left bunk, Kelly, says, breaking off Martin's reverie. "Them Brits have a funny way of trying to cheer up their blokes, songs about blackouts and broads back home," Kelly adds.

Martin looks out the corner of his eye to see who Kelly is talking to. Him apparently. Martin shrugs and rifles around in the bed clothes for the missing envelopes. For him "When the lights go on again" has a whole different meaning.

"On the floor," the tenured inpatient on the other side says. "You threw them there. I'd give you a hand, but I seem to have already donated," he laughs at the morbid joke at his own expense. He holds up his foreshortened arms to make the point.

Martin turns to see Louis, both limbs amputated at the elbows, and quickly looks away, averting his eyes to the floor under the pretence of trying to locate the letters.

A nurse uniformed in white cap and ward dress with a blue and maroon cap sweeps in on her way to anywhere else, humming a few bars of the song on the radio ending dramatically with, "Then we'll have time for things like wedding rings and free hearts will sing, When the lights go on again all over the world." She stoops to pick up the mail lying on the floor.

Martin likes Colleen and her irreverent sense of humor. Always singing. Probably helps in her line of work to joke with the men on her ward. One day as she was singing "I'm in the Mood for Love," one of her patients remarked sotto voce, "Boy, has she come to the right place!" Still, she has always shown great compassion to him, especially in her overnight shift during his nocturnal battle with demons real and imagined.

She plops the letters unceremoniously on the bed and says, "Well, I'm off for two whole days leave. Gonna miss me? I wanta get you guys' signatures for my autograph book since you might not be here when I get back."

Doubtful, Martin thinks.

Assuming she needs their John Hancock on some medical forms in triplicate, none of the men on the floor rush to be first. She thrusts a clipboard holding a two-dollar bill with scribbles all over it toward the obviously unarmed man.

"You first, Louie Armstrong."

He looks at the clipboard perplexed. "I fear I've left my piana playin' days behind me." He eyes the names written all over the bill. "How on earth am I," he begins when she sticks a stubby pencil in his mouth, flat side first.

"An X'll do from you," Colleen smiles and winks. "Don't worry, I'll remember ya."

Pencil between his teeth he says, "Uh a, 'ose 'ings are 'ad 'uck." He spits the pencil out and repeats, "Nuh huh, those things are bad luck," he says, nodding to deuce before him.

"You superstitious or something?" she asks.

"Not super, but maybe a little . . . stitious," he jokes. "Bad luck, those."

She gives him a once over. "Too late. Come on, give ol' Tom a tick." He shrugs and opens his mouth. She reinserts the pencil and holds the clipboard to his face as he makes a jerky, unsteady cross across the face of Thomas Jefferson.

She moves on to Martin and flips through the post she had set on the bed. "Don't worry, you won't be the first Noel to receive a Dear John from his gal back home. Ha, first Noel, now that's funny," she guffaws at her own play on words. Noel knows this gal is not back home. He also knows the fact his girl wrote to him means just the opposite, that she will not give up on him. But Colleen has no way of knowing this, so he gives her some slack. He realizes in her own crude and frank way, she is trying to be encouraging. Martin holds out his hand.

"Just gimme the pencil," he says, examining the autographed bill. Twenty-nine signatures and an X. In a moment of levity, he makes his own joke. "Looks like I am the first Noel," he announces, scrawling his name across the back, sideways.

The nurse goes down the row of beds, hounding each patient to autograph her "two for a dollar" bill, as she calls it.

"Whatcha gonna do with this here souvenir," a guy by the door asks, handing the clipboard to her. He is a lucky one, admitted for a ruptured appendix.

"Same thing I do with all the two-dollar bills in my pay envelope. When they're full of names, put 'em in a shoe box. Savin' 'em up. Gonna be filthy, stinkin' rich when this filthy, stinkin,' war is over." Reaching the end of the row, she opens the swinging door to leave. The men catch a few lines of another signature song crackling and popping as it plays on the vinyl 33. At the top of her lungs, Colleen sings along with Vera Lynn, "We'll meet again, don't know how, don't know when," before the doors close behind her.

## WE INTERRUPT THIS NOVEL TO BRING YOU THE TRUE STORY OF THOMAS JURVEVICH

Thomas grew up in the Jurjevich household, the son of Croatian immigrants. As such, the family's social standing was on par with those living in the Black community at the time. Regarded as "dirty immigrants," the Croatian families competed amongst themselves and other marginalized groups for the least desirable and lowest paying jobs.

This hardscrabble upbringing as the son of a coal miner, living adjacent to and on the wrong side of the railroad tracks, led Tom to leave home at 16. He joined a traveling circus, where he took up boxing. Proving to be pretty good at this, his job was to "take on all comers" when the circus came to town. If he won, money and food were his reward. This proved a "helluva motivator," in the words of Tom's youngest son, Mark. If he lost, Jurjevich moved on to the next bout, leaner, meaner, and less likely to lose.

Fed up and hungry after circus life, Tom joined the Merchant Marine, an allied organization staffed by civilian mariners aboard civilian and federal merchant vessels. This service took him across the globe and "up the Yangtze River around the time when the Japanese began their age-old tradition of kicking the hell out of the Chinese," according to Mark. Sensing something bigger was brewing and considering the eventual likelihood of the U.S. participation in the European war, Jurjevich and a buddy finished their last run with the Merchant Marine and enlisted in the United States Marine Corps.

As they were already in the East, on that side of the world, the two were trained in Hawaii at the naval base there. As luck(?) would have it, (Mark's emphasis, not mine), "Pearl Harbor turned into quite the hot spot in world politics." One Sunday morning, Thomas was just leaving Mass when the first planes appeared. Oddly it was a minute or two before sirens sounded, mostly because no one believed it.

The invading forces clearly had intel on the island's operations. As Jurjevich was running to the harbor, he passed oil storage reservoirs that had been emptied only a couple nights before. Fearing these would be bombed and he would be torched with them, Jurjevich hit the ground as Imperial Japanese aircraft dove in. Uncannily, the bombers skipped the depleted reservoirs and hit the ones to which the oil had been moved.

The air was full of burning ships, explosions and "the smell of oil and death," Mark remembers his father saying. After the onslaught ended, the American troops, shell shocked, angry, and demoralized, were still on full alert, fearful of a ground invasion that never came.

After serving on a ship, Jurjevich was assigned to a special unit in that theater of operations, the Marine Raider. Used mostly in the Solomon Island campaign, these were guerilla single man operations, put on islands behind enemy lines with a raft, a .45 caliber weapon, a knife and a radio. They were to live off the land, avoid detection, and kill silently while radioing back enemy positions and ship locations that usually moved at night.

Mark remembers hearing how his father and other Raiders would compare notes on how they killed without a sound. The risks were high. The

Japanese weren't particularly tied to the Geneva Convention, he said, so tactics used against captured soldiers usually began with ripping out their fingernails, toenails, or teeth. This sometimes escalated to their literally being skinned alive. Jurjevich was witness to at least one such event. Outmanned and outgunned, the Marine Raider could do nothing about it.

These horrors and the experiences that followed shaped his post-war personality.

On a destroyer about to storm "some no-name island" when his ship came under attack, Jurjevich was blasted from the ship. Once in the water, he made it ashore, taking position behind a log. As he was firing back at the enemy, a round from a machine gun loaded with dum-dum (shrapnel) bullets clipped the knuckle on his little finger and pinged three shots down his right shin.

Losing blood and consciousness, he held a knife to his own throat determined not to go out by the hand of the Japanese....but he passed out.

Jurjevich awoke in a makeshift bamboo prison of sorts...more just stakes in the ground held together with wire and grenades. The island was still under assault, and judging by the dwindling personnel in the camp, the Japanese were losing. When it got down to one prison guard, one of the prisoners, an exceptionally large black man who was being held with Jurjevich, reached through the bars, grabbed the neck of the last remaining soldier, and snapped it, allowing the men to make an escape. Jurjevich was in no condition to do so though.

This giant of a man, whose foot had been broken either before or during the escape, packed Jurjevich over rough terrain on his shoulder for some distance until they located a storage area near a small river. He placed Jurjevich in an empty 55-gallon barrel and kicked him out to sea, where he bobbed along until someone on a nearby ship noticed the drum. A man named Malhalovich pulled him aboard, rescuing Jurjevich.

When Jurjevich awoke on the medical ship days later, the big man with the broken foot, the one who had saved him by carrying him from the makeshift prison and then set him out to sea, was berthed in the bunk next to him. In another amazing turn of events, after their postwar return to civilian life, Mahalovich, the man who found Jurjevich and pulled him out of the water, lived down the street in the same town, St. Joseph, Missouri. "So all in all, a happy ending," Mark said.

But before returning to that life though, Jurjevich, injured and traumatized, was deemed unsuited to return to the battlefield so he joined the War Bonds Tour as a veteran and traveled stateside as a speaker. After his time abroad, he met a young Navy cadet bound for service in the W.A.V.E.S. -- Women Accepted for Volunteer Emergency Service -- a division of the U.S. Navy created during World War II. She was stationed as a secretary in the Intelligence Department. Following a whirlwind romance, she and Staff Sergeant Thomas Jurjevich, who was still recuperating from his service in the South Pacific, married in New Orleans. To this union, nine children were born. The family changed their surname, for convenience and in court, from

Jurjevich to Justin for the sake of their children to better assimilate after the war. According to Mark Justin, their youngest, reflecting on his father's legacy, "The mental effect this war had on many of the men was largely overlooked in the post war. Jimmy Stewart, in *It's a Wonderful Life*...when he's yelling at the kids and his wife...that scene.... later it was disclosed that he was in a full-fledged PTSD attack. I'm sure the horrors of war begat demons a-plenty among men in that era."

Incidentally, Mark Justin's daughter prefers to use the original family name, Jurjevich.

## VIGNETTE SEVEN

### JUNE

### "Yankee Doodle Dandy"

At first glance, the safe deposit box that lay open on the table did not appear to contain much in the way of contents. A small American flag, a harmonica, a Bible the size of a deck of cards, a guide of some sort, a tiny red address book, a few yellowed newspaper clippings, and a steno-type notebook that was bound at the top rather than the old side spiral type Leigh remembered seeing. On top of it all was a portrait studio of a dark-haired beauty. Her grandmother, of that she was sure.

Even though Leigh didn't remember a time Granny Vivi's hair was not silver, the smiling eyes were unmistakable. Even when she passed at 103, she still had those bright friendly eyes. She always had a happy countenance despite having lost Grandpa Stan, Vivi's husband of 56 years, decades earlier, and having outlived her two youngest daughters who had each passed within a few years of one another in their 70s. With their deaths it was incumbent on Leigh's mother, the oldest of the three sisters, to make all the necessary arrangements on her own.

So when Leigh volunteered to help in any way possible, Verna had asked her to go to the bank and close out the long forgotten safe deposit account.

Leigh took the items out of the long metal tray and laid them on the table one by one for a cursory inventory. She wasn't sure what she was looking at or for, but her grandmother's effects had contained a bank box key so here she was. Her family had banked here since Noah was in knee britches, as her grandmother would say, so she wondered how long it had been since these items had seen the light of day. Surely they had paid an annual maintenance fee to keep a box that seemed to contain nothing of great value. Leigh didn't know what to expect, but for her mother's sake she was hoping for a stack of hundred-dollar bills or a stock certificate worth millions. When she had mentioned her hopes to Verna, her mother had said, "Highly improbable, but thank you for doing this for me." Leigh's grandparents had farmed a piece of land that her mother would now inherit. It had a Century Farm sign by the driveway to indicate it had been in the Sherwood family a very long time. After Grandpa died, Grandma Vivi rented the land to a neighbor who grazed cattle and raised hay, which helped pay the taxes and for a small bungalow in town where Grandma lived alone until most recently. Then rather than go into assisted living, Verna had moved Vivian in with her to save money, and they both enjoyed the company.

Leigh inspected each article before her in turn. The flag she noted had only 48 stars, so, pre-1950s. She blew into the harmonica, producing a discordant honk, and then inhaled to create an equally painful wail. She looked around in embarrassment to see if any alarmed bank employees came running. No one did. The King James Pocket Bible contained only the New Testament. Inside the cover she learned that it had been presented to Grandpa, Stanley Sherwood, in 1944 by the Women's League and signed by its president, Mrs. Arthur Wagers. Leigh shook her head in wonder at a time women self-identified by their husband's name. The guide was kind of a catch all book for soldiers and sailors, part-hymnal part Boy Scout handbook. "God Bless America" meets "Yankee Doodle Dandy."

The itty-bitty red book captured her attention. "Compliments of the Red Cross" was embossed on its cover. Best she could tell, this was a mid-century contact list. Inside were a couple dozen names written in a combination of cramped hands, along with mailing addresses and phone numbers, or so she guessed. The street addresses contained different state abbreviations than the two capitalized letters she was accustomed to. And all were missing zip codes. She marveled that something addressed only Vernon Porter, 425 Second, Wamego, Kans. would be sufficient for delivery.

But the craziest of all were the phone numbers. Each of them contained words or prefixes, she guessed. She couldn't imagine how one would even begin to send a text to someone on those old rotary payphones using these numbers. You probably had to talk to the operator whose name was Elsie or Betsy, she imagined with a snort.

Leigh moved on to the notebook next. When she lifted its cover, the cover and the pages all came undone. She made a mental note to be careful to make sure the pages didn't get out of order in case there was supposed to be an order.

The top of the first page said, "Dear Baby." Oh good, this was going to be a juicy letter. "I know you won't read this any time soon." Leigh was hooked already.

*learn. I havn't heard if you are a boy or girl, but all the boys want me to call you by their name. Wise guys. Don't worry I won't let anyone name you after any of these galoots. Back again. Our boat has women on it. I tell you this on account you might be a girl. This makes the boys act twitterpated, which you will learn when you get big. I only have eyes for Vivian so you got nothing to worry about. The women some are nurses some are WACS. Aside me Jonny is married and his wife is what they call a Rosie cept her name is actually Anna Mae. She welds if you can believe it. Girls are doing near everything the guys always done these days. It's a good thing I guess. Me again. We got some colored fellas on our ship. Nice guys but I can't understand their talk much. Many trained mechanics. We all get together and play music. Now that's a language we all speak the same. There are some band instruments on the boat and some of the boys brought fiddles. The West Point has its own piano. Vern plays like nobodies business. The piano stays in a funny shaped crate that opens in the front because it will be stationed like us in Europe. The North Atlantic is rough with storms but we try to keep our minds off the stormy weather and whatalls coming. We play cards and music. It's the only time we see the girls. They stay together in a bunch but listen to us play on an upper deck. We take requests and they drop nickels on us for playing their song. We can tell they are jitterbugging but don't have a good view. I'm more used to music from the Grand Ol' Opry but one new song that I learned that is real funny is Mairzy Doats. You and your momma will have to listen for it on the radio. The boys wish for more fraternization but it is not permitted. Makes no nevermind to me because I got you and my girl back home. I wish I knew whether you was a Miss or a Mister but time for all that later. I just keep adding lines on this tablet to save space each day. Today we road up the River Clyde. Then went to South Hampton by train. When we got on a LST to cross the Channel, the C.O. almost missed the boat and had to be pulled aboard by rope. He is called Bates but we call him Lates. We put ashore on Utah Beach. That's in Normandy, France. One day you will study all about what happened on this beach. I bet a dollar. We were assigned to a battalion in Paris. We assembled in a field 5 miles from the beach. Bates went on some sight seeing trip of the other beaches and left us to fend for our own selfs. We camped for 3 days while he was gone on recon with only the food we took from the ship's larder. While we remained unassigned to a battalion we could not draw rations. Bates finally showed up. Jonny said better Lates than never. Boy did we have appetite by then. We attached to our battalion in Cherbourg. Red Ball Transfer transported us and our equipment with their trucks including that funny shaped box. We cheered that we got to keep the crate with the matching piano. Vern is happy. They divied our company into two halves. I had 600 to 1800 shift. The other guys were all on 1800 to 600.*

*A few weeks ago, maybe months I lost track, I finally got the letter that Vivian's mother sent a long time back. It had the two newspaper clippings. Today is V-E day but I am still too sad to make merry. Though I never met you, I loved you and love you still. You will always be my little boy.*

# WE INTERRUPT THIS NOVEL TO BRING YOU YET ANOTHER ENTIRELY TRUE ACCOUNT, THAT OF THEODORE H. SCHOON

## VIGNETTE EIGHT

## JULY

### "The Star-Spangled Banner"

C O N F I D E N T I A L

<u>HEADQUARTERS 34TH INFANTRY DIVISION</u>

UNITED STATES ARMY

APO-34

To    : Corporal Theodore H. Schoon, 37037453, Company "M", 135th Infantry Regiment.

Thru   : Commanding Officer, 135th Infantry Regiment.

CWR/LAB/pa

8 March 1944

1. Under the provisions of AR 600-45 and as announced in General orders No. 18, Headquarters 34th Infantry Division, dated 7 March 1944, a Silver Star is awarded to the following individual:

       Theodore H. Schoon, 37037453, Company "M", 135th Infantry Regiment. For gallantry in action on 3 December 1943, in the vicinity of Selvone, Italy. When his platoon was subjected to a particularly severe enemy artillery barrage Cpl. Schoon although he had already passed through the area in which most of the shells were falling, Corporal Theodore H. Schoon, with utter disregard for his own safety, returned to the danger area and carried a fellow who had been wounded to a place of safety. Following this, he again went back to the area, which was still under fire, and stayed at this voluntary post to act as a guide for the men of his company that had been cut off from the rest of his battalion as a result of the shelling. Corporal Schoon's outstanding courage and initiative in risking his own life for the benefit of his fellow comrades was an inspiration to the entire company and a credit to the Armed Forces of the United States. Entered service from: George, Iowa.

Charles W. Ryder
Major General, U.S. Army
Commanding

## C O N F I D E N T I A L

When Corporal Ted Schoon received a commendation marked "confidential," he took to heart the admonition to keep secret the actions he took on behalf of his wounded comrades for the next fifty years. Although news of the awarding of a Silver Star plus other medals for gallantry was printed in his hometown newspaper during his deployment overseas, it was the Army, and not Corporal Schoon, who notified them of this account. Perhaps his humble and dutiful nature was instilled in him by the same German heritage that inspired the actions that led to these very accolades. For it was in service of the Schoon's German-speaking family's adopted country that Ted fought against the Army of the Third Reich.

The fact remains, it was not until shortly before his passing that Ted spoke of the events that earned him the Silver Star, as well as the combat infantryman badge and three campaign stars on his European theater ribbon. So humble was Ted Schoon, his youngest daughter only heard of her father's heroics when, as a girl after piano lessons one day, her paternal grandmother, who didn't want her son to know, showed her the *Sioux City Journal* clippings she had kept in her possession and close to her heart over the years.

One account listed the exacting standards of the decoration recently authorized by the War Department, which included having proven his fighting ability in combat, and went so far as to describe the medal as "the handsome badge set against a background of infantry blue, enclosed in a silver wreath." The gilt-toned star of five points has on the obverse side in the center, a small silver star, centered within a wreath of laurel. Eighteen rays radiate from the star to the wreath. The reverse of the star has the inscription: "For Gallantry in Action" in raised letters, below which is a blank area suitable for engraving the recipient's name. Ted never bothered having his name engraved in the provided space. This was not out of any disrespect for the country that bestowed it, but rather out of a sense of selflessness and duty that led men of his generation to make such sacrifices. Their service, which in many cases amounted to years out of their prime for the duration of the war, was part and parcel of this allegiance.

The ribbon on which the star hung was considered one of the most striking of all the American awards. Featuring a wide red center stripe flanked on either side by stripes of dark blue and white in varying widths, the Silver Star was indeed a handsome badge. Regardless, Ted, like many recipients from among our country's Greatest Generation, put the box that contained the emblem, our nation's recognition of his valor, in his sock drawer.

Ted's daughter continued her piano lessons, learning to play the hymns and patriotic tunes her father favored. When she grew up, his daughter shared the story of her father's bravery with her husband, and it was to him that his father-in-law opened up about his time in the service. Ted's wife of fifty-plus years and his daughter, seated at the dining room table eating homemade ice cream on the Fourth of July, overheard Ted tell his son-in-law about his time in the Army. Perhaps it was the younger man's experience in law enforcement that allowed Ted to share the occurrences of a half-century earlier as to a fellow comrade-in - arms.

The two had taken their bowls of hand-cranked vanilla ice cream to the parlor, as they termed it, to eat as the women washed up after dinner. The town fireworks would begin after dark. As they waited for the municipal band to begin playing the national anthem, the signal the annual patriotic aerial display would soon begin, Ted spoke of his time as an infantryman attached to the Red Bull Division. The younger man knew Ted had risen to the rank of Communications Sergeant but that night he learned how Ted survived three campaigns on two continents and lived to finally tell another human being, with two others listening in, about his part in the effort that led to Victory in Europe and helped put an end to World War II.

## VOICE EIGHT

## NORTH AMERICA, UNITED KINGDOM, NORTH AFRICA, EUROPE

## 1941-1945

### "Just As I Am"

Inducted in the spring of 1941 mere months before the United States joined the war, Private Theodore Schoon enlisted and was sent to Camp Claiborne for basic training. Along with 7000 others, Ted slogged through the muck and mire of Louisiana swamp country to train amidst snakes and chiggers in humidity and heat. The men billeted in tents, so great was the effort to house what might become a fighting force should Hitler's actions draw America into the war that had begun in Europe two years earlier. The unprovoked attack on Pearl Harbor, however, forced a change in the nation's tide of events and prompted Roosevelt to declare war. What was to have been a one-year National Guard enlistment for Ted and his company suddenly became a much longer deployment as soldiers in the United States Army. During a brief leave before shipping out, Ted proposed to his girl mere days before he shipped overseas.

Ted's military service, which began in North America, would take him first across the Atlantic to the United Kingdom. Along with the usual Government Issue trappings of a soldier, Ted also went armed with a military edition of a King James New Testament and a copy of *Song and Service Book for Ship and Field*. This manual included such familiar hymns as "What a Friend We Have in Jesus" and "Just As I Am." It was without one plea and secure in his knowledge of his Savior that Ted embarked on what he had no way of knowing would be a three-year expedition spanning thousands of nautical and geographic miles to hell and back. Also included in the song book were the patriotic standards of Katharine Lee Bates and Samuel Francis Smith. Even after he realized the cost of such allegiance, "America the Beautiful" and "My Country Tis of Thee" never failed to stir the Iowa farm boy's heart. But it was the smallest book that had the greatest significance to Ted. At all times to keep his bearings, Ted carried a miniature Red Cross address book like a compass pointing home. Filled with the names, mailing addresses, and telephone numbers of loved ones back in Iowa in his tidy script, the slim volume also bore the details for newly acquainted but lifelong friendships, the duration of which varied greatly from man to man.

Ted set sail from Brooklyn for Belfast. Unprepared as the U.S. was for such a large-scale mobilization of men and munitions, troops were transported in every seaworthy vessel available to them to various fronts. The luxury liner "The Queen Mary" was even called into service, and though Ted was initially set to sail on her, a last-minute fire aboard the magnificent passenger vessel meant crossing the North Atlantic on the "RMS Aquitania," considered the "half-sister of the Lusitania." Requisitioned for the war effort, the Cunard vessel zigzagged across the North Atlantic to avoid German U-boats traveling as wolf packs.

Once the troop ship arrived in Ireland, the uniformed occupants headed to a base for combat training. A member of one of the first selective service groups assigned to the 135th Infantry division of the 34th regiment Red Bulls, Ted joined the great flotilla heading to North Africa as a mortarman. Threading the Strait of Gibraltar, one of the fleet was struck by a torpedo, forcing 700 men to take to lifeboats in the middle of the night, making for an inauspicious start for what was being called "Operation Torch."

On the African front of the war, the Americans found Field Marshal Erwin Rommel's forces entrenched behind garrisons of timber and steel. The 135th infantry divided and captured Fonduck Pass from the Germans. For their efforts, men were afforded a single hot meal each day. It was a Pyrrhic victory of sorts, achieved at great cost in the number of fatalities and wounded.

In time the Allies had the "Desert Fox" on the run, and the Americans pursued Rommel's army 1,500 miles across the arid terrain. Their backs to the Mediterranean, the Army of the Third Reich, joined by their Italian Axis allies, dug in at a fortress of rock caves accessible only by goat trail in Tunisia. Behind a smoke screen, Germans sniped at American troops at Hill 609. Finally, flanked by the 135th and the 133rd with reinforcements in the form of French auxiliary units of ganja-smoking indigenous Moroccan Goumiers, Germany surrendered. One of these "Gomes" as they were called, told Ted that when he smoked the narcotic, his "head feel big, like a mule."

Seventy-five thousand Afrika Korp Expeditionary troops were taken prisoner following this pivotal battle in which over four thousand Red Bull troops were killed. Though depleted in number, the Red Bull earned a reputation for bravery and sacrifice that secured their foremost position leading the Fifth Army victory parade in Tunis.

After establishing a beachhead, the American forces joined the invasion in Italy on the other side of the Mediterranean. Back on the European front, the Red Bulls forded the frigid waters of the Volturno river. Men and machinery were lost during repeated crossings in the strong current during muddy and cold conditions. Waiting on the other side were the Nebelwerfer German six-barreled rocket mortars which became famous in the Italian campaign as "Screaming Meemies" or, as the 45th Division dubbed it, "Wailing Willie."

The persistence of the 135th paid off, and Panzer divisions gave up Hill 235, but not before scarring many who encountered the German onslaught, condemning them to a lifetime of nightmares of not knowing whether they were running away from or directly into the fray. On December 3, 1943, the nightmare was real. As Ted's confidential commendation reported, Corporal Schoon "with utter disregard for his own safety, returned to the danger area and carried a fellow who had been wounded to a place of safety." Then, he returned under fire to continue guiding men in his company to safety. Corporal Schoon's valor on behalf of his comrades was "an inspiration to the entire company and a credit to the Armed Forces of the United States." For this gallantry, Ted was awarded the Silver Star, which was pinned to his uniform by Lieutenant General Mark W. Clark, commander of Fifth Army U.S.A. in Italy on March 13, 1943.

The battle may have been won, but the war was far from over. During a brutal winter in 1944, the 135th was tasked with an attack on two Italian cities as part of an effort to wrest the sixth-century Benedictine abbey, Monte Cassino, from German control. Considered a holy shrine, the abbey was home to priceless art and sculptures, as well as thought to house soldiers of the Third Reich.

After several skirmishes in which the Red Bull division was repelled due to a lack of reinforcements, one platoon breached the abbey and apprehended 14 German prisoners found hiding in a cave. U.S. high command sent B-17s to bombard the abbey, an unpopular decision, as the abbey was not only considered sacred and a sanctuary, but also was home to centuries of cultural treasures. Over time, and with the might of five divisions, the Italian abbey and its contents were utterly destroyed in May.

At least one relic survived the shelling. A Roman Catholic nurse attached to their battalion salvaged a small-scale alabaster sculpture of Mary and the infant Christ Child from the rubble. She imagined perhaps it came from the cloistered cell of a Benedictine nun and kept it as a talisman.

The Liberators continued their fight toward Rome, where in June 1944 they marched through the streets as celebrated victors, putting an end to Axis tyranny and ultimately leading to total Victory in Europe. Of his role in the global events that changed the geopolitical landscape, Ted told his son-in-law, "The day you realize you are going to die is the day you become a soldier."

For this Greatest of Generations, their eventual return home would bring a return to civilian life. By Independence Day the following year, Ted was back on the farm, married to his sweetheart, and beginning life anew. Armed with memories that most endured in silence, legions of servicemen likewise quietly resumed the life they had put on hold - - except on those rare occasions when they broke silence, chiefly in the company of men still living such as those listed in the tiny red Red Cross address book.

```
BE STRONG!
    Be strong!
We are not here to play—to dream,
    to drift.
We have hard work to do and loads
    to lift.
Shun not the struggle—face it; 'tis
    God's gift.

    Be strong!
Say not the days are evil. Who's to
    blame?
And fold the hands and acquiesce—
    O shame!
Stand up, speak out, and bravely,
    in God's name.

    Be strong!
It matters not how deep intrenched
    the wrong,
How hard the battle goes, the day
    how long;
Faint not—fight on! Tomorrow
    comes the song.
            —Maltbie D. Babcock.
```

*Having travelled to Europe and Africa with him, this poem was found clipped inside Schoon's Red Cross book.

## VIGNETTE NINE

## AUGUST

### "Taps"

"Hey, over here!" Matt yelled. The teenager pointed to the ground. The day was not unduly warm for August, and the gentle breeze made it almost pleasant.

His sisters came from the other side of the newly dedicated Four County Veterans Memorial brick yard in the center of the city park.

"Jenny, go get Uncle Mel out of the car," Katie said.

"Dad, over here," Katie called to her father who was reading names listed on the bronze Vietnam tablet.

"They did a nice job putting this all together," Christine, Mike's wife, said, short of breath from her jaunt from the American flag in the center of the park. "I found some Winstons and some Darnells listed as far back as World War I."

Mike and Christine and their son Matt and daughter Katie stood waiting as Jenny patiently walked alongside Uncle Mel as he made his way from the car. Refusing the aid of a walker or cane, he slowly progressed in their general direction, stopping to take in names inscribed on the pavers at his feet. Although he lived less than a mile away at the state veterans' home, he had not been out to see the memorial until now. At age 98, his license had been suspended so he relied on family members for outings.

"That guy worked at our grocery store," he commented, nodding in the direction of a Clifford Sample. "After he came home from Korea," he added, pronouncing it KO-rea, "become a butcher. Took over his old man's store. Best ham salad you ever tasted."

He pointed out one after another of the red bricks, each engraved with name, rank, and range-of-service dates. One commemorative stone in particular arrested him. Finally, he spoke. "This here's my cousin on my mother's side," Uncle Mel said to Jenny, looking upon the stone for a Loren Brockhurst. "Left a wife and two little kiddies. He was such a card. Never forget he shipped out a few months before I did. Was walking by the house and stopped to wave through the window at us sittin' at the table. Smiled real big at us all. We were havin' supper. Didn't say a word, just smiled. Killed at Iwo Jima. You seen that statue of those guys raising the flag? That's Iwo Jima. Brutal. We always talked about how he stopped by, didn't come in or nothin,' just waved big and grinned. Got a granddaughter named for him, Lorna. She's a preacher for the Methodists."

Uncle Mel continued his journey with Jenny only to suddenly come to a halt once again. "That guy barely missed Pearl Harbor. Stationed there but out to sea that Sunday. Lucky S.O.B, you ask me," he reflected. "Still owes me three dollars from a game of poker. Guess that score's settled." He turned to spit and to make his way to the waiting family but was stopped by another brick.

"I knew Lt. Colonel Knagee there all my life. From when he was wearing knee britches. Went to Burma. There's a picture of him wearing short pants sitting with some other fellas, officer types, all dressed in white. Not sure what he had against long pants. It's up at the VFW on the wall."

"I bet Clyde Morgan's even here somewhere abouts," he said, peering around.

"Now who was that?" Jenny asked, taking the old man's arm to steer him in the direction of the waiting family. She was merely making conversation and at first not really paying attention to what he was saying.

"Good frienda your grandpa and mine. Drove a General every day to the Nuremberg trials. Had very little to say about the whole affair but I knew it grated on him, watching those Nazis on the stand. Lasted almost a year. Seeing those pictures. Auschwitz and all that. Nasty business. Hanged the worst of the lot. Said they was just following orders. It ate at him, it did. Told me something that always stuck with him. And it always stuck with me. He said one of the prosecutors at the trials, little Jewish fella, said war makes murderers out of otherwise decent people, all wars, all decent people."

Jenny was paying attention now. Uncle Mel stood lost in thought. Then he shook it off. "But Clyde, he tried to put all that behind him. Had a nice family. Lots of kids. Catholic. Musta died five, seven years back."

As if on cue, a lone bugler began to blow "Taps." A gathering of people in the distance laid a wreath near a monument commemorating more recent war dead, those from a Middle East deployment. Uncle Mel held his salute throughout the presentation, although it was happening 100 yards away. When it was over, the somber spell lifted.

Jenny and Uncle Mel walked several steps, and he started to laugh. "Good time Charlie. Quit engineer school at Rolla right after Pearl and up and enlisted. Worked his way up and become an ensign. We played cards together and we all remembered how the native women in the South Seas went about, pardon my language, but with bare breasts. Well one day, ol Charlie give one the women a undershirt, and danged if she didn't cut two holes it. Said it was too tight across the udders!"

Melvin doubled over in laughter at the thought, and Jenny blushed but had to laugh with him. "Got half his mustache shot off one time," he continued. "Standing on the deck of the *Oakland* during a battle and a bullet whizzed by and clipped his whiskers. Least to hear him tell. Shaved off the rest and never grew one again. Had the funniest stories. Not sure I believed them all. Could drink anyone under the table though."

Still amused by thoughts of Good Time Charlie, Uncle Mel came into the home stretch. "Bunch of my old friends are here," he announced as he approached the waiting family. They smiled wanly and looked at the ground before them. The only sound came from the groundskeeper's mower. Uncle Mel took note of their somber expressions.

"Ah, there you are, Buddy," Melvin sighed, seeing the tribute brick for his youngest brother at their feet. Beneath the name the inscription read *1731st Tech 5* and an end-of-service date, *1945*. "Mike, 'course you wasn't even born, but I sure wish you coulda met your dad in about 1944. He woulda been about Matt's age." The old man saluted the stone, brushing his hand across his eyes. "He was an entirely different person, but he came home and made the best of it."

"I asked him once why he didn't try to pursue compensation or disability. The VA told him time and again he had a case," Mike said. "Back in those days they didn't know as much about head injuries and PTSD."

"Buddy never said too much, but he was proud to have served and understood anything could happen. Saw service as his duty and didn't want to profit from it," Uncle Mel explained.

After a few minutes, they turned without talking to head back toward the car. Passing rows upon rows of red memorial stones marked with names and dates, Mike said, "It's like these bricks laid the foundation for the better part of the twentieth century."

"*Better part* is right," said Uncle Mel. "Not sure why an old codger like me is still on this side of the sod. I'm ready for when my Maker decides my time's up."

**VOICE NINE**

**THE PACIFIC, AUGUST 1945**

**"This Land Is Your Land"**

Looking over Boyle's shoulder at duty assignments, Winston says, "Will ya look at that." The maintenance mechanic wipes his hands on a greasy rag and stuffs it in his pocket.

"What?" asks Walker angling for a better view of the bulletin board. As a member of the military police, he was always insinuating himself into situations. Winston points at the notice typed single-space on an index card. Walker reads: "Ordnance aboard Superfortress Enola Gay launched 08-Aug from Tinian has been dropped on Hiroshima. Another bomb aboard Bockscar launched 09-Aug hit Nagasaki. It is projected these bombs will bring about an end to hostilities and a declaration of surrender, ending the war."

"Hey, I worked on that plane," Boyle, the newly appointed crew chief, states matter of factly. He takes a bite of his Spamwich.

"Which one?" asks Winston.

"Both actually," Boyle concludes, mouth full. "Different times though. Been weeks ago."

"There is no way," Walker declares, headed for the hangar door for the rest of his shift as M.P. During daylight hours there was little to patrol on the island but once night fell the drunk and disorderlies came to life.

"Whatever," Boyle states indifferently, drinking a Coke to wash down his lunch.

"No, I believe you," Walker says. "I just can't see how they can say two measly bombs will end the war," he adds for clarification. He looks at the pinup calendar with a blonde bombshell hanging by a tack near the overhead door. "It's the 12th. You'd think we'da heard something by now."

Boyle laughs, shielding his eyes from the bright sun, "Pack your bags, boys. We're going home! NYC, here I come!"

"Maybe I'll be home before my 20th birthday," Winston considers, his boots kicking an empty coconut husk beneath his feet. "I hope my girl is still waiting for me."

"Is she twelve, or is she younger than you?" Walker jokes. "Besides, you just got here, kid. Maybe with any luck you'll be back in time for harvest though, eh, plowboy? Maybe even beat your brothers home."

"Wouldn't that be something. Mom'll sure be happy. She was none too glad when I left school early and enlisted."

"And that left nine people in your graduating class, including your little girlfriend," snorts Walker to no reply.

"That 'cause you fibbed 'bout your age?" Boyle inquires, ignoring Walker.

"No. Mom said the postmaster said I didn't have to go on account I'm the youngest. Mom had her hands full with the garden and such so she worried about the farm and having all her sons overseas. Uncle Sam wouldn't leave the farm to run its ownself, she said. But I talked my cousin into taking over the chores for me. He was 4F on account he has flat feet."

"Where's your dad figure in all this?" Boyle asks.

"He never made it back from the last war. Well, his body did but he was never the same. Shell-shocked. Died when I was a little-bitty kid," Winston explains.

"Your brothers all Army?" asks Boyle.

"All 'cept Melvin. Other two in Europe somewhere. Mel is a turret gunner on the U.S.S. Manila Bay," Winton says. "Actually ran into him one time. Can you believe that, all the way from home in the middle of the Pacific. Our ships are in this port, and I hear this voice say, 'Hey Boy-O! Hey Buddy Boy!' That's what they called me round home, Buddy. Didn't even have time to get together for a drink," Winston reflects. "I got it good here in this tropical oasis, if you can believe it," he says, taking in his surroundings. "He's the one I worry about. Helluva dangerous job, turret man."

"Yea, this is paradise alright. See you guys around. That is unless the war's actually won and we get to leave Shangry La," Walker says as they part for the day's duties.

*January 15, 1946*

*Dear Mrs. Winston,*

*I know by now you have likely heard through official channels about Marvin and that he's coming home. One time when we were talking, Marvin told me about his brothers and his kin back home, so I thought I should write to you. I recalled the name of the town he told me you lived near, and so I hope this letter finds you well. I am with him in the hospital just now. I am writing you because I am sure Marvin has no recollection of what even happened.*

*After the events of the first week in August, a bunch of us guys including Marvin were sent plumb to N------ from T---- for a major cleanup detail. We ran construction equipment to clear the path for reconstruction. One day Marvin and me went with our buddy Walker who was a M.P. to pick up a prisoner. Winston, by which I mean Marvin, agreed to go on patrol with us to bring this detainee back to the brig. It had been raining that night, and the roads were beyond terrible. Not only was there debris, but now slick with mud plus lightning. Marvin, Walker, the prisoner and me were all in a open jeep between sheer drop offs on either side. Walker was always pretty sure of his driving and was probably going too fast for the conditions. Walker veered to miss something in the road and the Jeep flipped and rolled down the embankment. When I came to I knew I had a broke arm and collar bone plus a crushed knee. Walker had some busted ribs. We was afeard Marvin was gone. The prisoner was dead.*

*Two days later, someone realized they were missing a prisoner, so the brig sent out a search party. It took a few days, but they finally got us to a field hospital. Funny thing is, by now the war was over. We made it through the fighting with nary a scratch only to nearly get killed after V-J Day. Well, I did do a dumb stunt on a beach once and got hurt, but that was my own fault. I learned that Marvin was alive but still unconscious. As he was hanging on but was still out of it, once the swell went down they done a surgery to put a metal plate to cover the gash in his head. A lot like we use to do when we fixed airplanes that had took some flack, now that I think of it.*

*With the war being over, between my bum wing and bad knee, they kicked me loose. Marvin is being discharged as well. It is honorable and like to earn him some gongs. I asked could I accompany him back to the States. They granted leave for that just now so we can travel together.*

*Reason I'm writing is to prepare your hearts somewhat. Your boy is coming home, but he's a different man. Use to be fun-loving and chatty, but he's more quiet like now. He has no memory of the accident and I had to work to get him to remember me even. Tell the truth, I'm not right sure he does but he is at least agreeable and seemed to know me when I had them bring him a birthday cake. The headaches give him fits something awful though. Bout the only thing that seems to relieve them somewhat is gentle music. Nothing too loud. We got a piano here and a chaplain plays hymns and some U.S. of A. songs. He smiles when the padre plays "This Land is Your Land." I think he remembers it from home. I know he has a girl back there. Best she be prepared for his return too.*

*We should be home in the coming weeks. I sure hope your other boys are also out of harm's way. I'll cable to let you know when to pick him up at the station. I'm from the East, but I will go as far as Union Station to see that he gets to Kansas City okay. I wish I had more welcome news, but I thought you might want to prepare yourself and make ready for Marvin's return.*

*Sincerely,*

*Corporal Michael Boyle*

*US Army*

## VIGNETTE TEN

## A CONVERSATION WITH MERLE GREEN

## & EARL MCKINNEY

I had an opportunity to visit with two World War II veterans in the veterans home just across town from me. **Merle Green** (102) was a Winston, Missouri, farm boy who, along with his three brothers, served overseas. When he left for the service, his dad, who was always suspicious of the flying machines, said, "Stay away from airplanes."

Despite this admonition, as a crew chief and flight engineer in the "Far East by way of Hawaii," Merle spent WW II aboard the C-47. This transport plane, nicknamed the Gooney Bird, was also known as the Flying Coffin. To confirm, I said, "That's the plane that towed the gliders, right?"

"Yes, ma'am," he answered. The C-47 also dropped thousands of paratroopers on D-Day. Merle shared stories of working on a parachute squadron. One time an officer about to jump from a plane turned to Merle and said, "Now this is perfectly safe, isn't it?" The officer's ripcord got caught up in the static line, and Merle had to untangle him. "I reached up and got to thinking, what am I doing? I ain't got a parachute! But I reached for the line and got him loose. He gave me a football shove, knocking me down, and turned to waved. When I saw him on the ground later. I said, 'You get scared?' He said, 'I didn't have time to be scared.'"

Merle said his brothers were mobilized to all fronts of the war. One of the things that amused him was being told if they come under fire to dig a foxhole. "You don't dig a foxhole in coral," he laughed.

Merle survived not one but three wars and showed me photographs and certificates from his 23 years of service. Family photos around the room showed a life well-lived and greatly loved.

Given his age, Merle is a bit difficult to hear, and it isn't easy for him to hear listeners. He said something about a WAC with whom he had corresponded for two years. "She was in a different squadron than I was." I teased him a little and asked if she was his sweetheart. He gave a laugh and looked at me with an impish grin. Then his countenance grew serious. "I went to high school with her. We always went to dance and WFC. She was a grade behind me. I left for overseas and wrote to her for over two years. I finally got back home. I called her up and said, 'Rose, is there someplace we can talk, be quiet. I heard the hotels around here . . . for dinner. I met her at the Savoy there, had a big kiss. We walked over to the table to sit down.. She opened her pocketbook, said 'I must show you this.' She had MARRIED while I . . ." He stopped speaking.

"She was married?" I asked, not having expected this development.

"Yeah."

"Who'd she marry?"

"I don't know. I never did meet him. I just got up and left. But she said back in Kansas City.

It hurt but you gotta find out about it before it's too late."

Just then the social worker who had coordinated our visit came to the door. As I was leaving, Merle grabbed my hand. He said, "I touched one of the atom bombs. Big Boy." Knowing "Fat Man" and "Little Boy" were dropped by Enola Gay and Bockscar on Hiroshima and Nagasaki respectively, I wasn't sure to which he referred. But all these years later he was struck by the devastation of those bombs, which was evident over a decade later when he returned to the area. "Nobody ever could live there years later."

As we were leaving, something else occurred to Merle so he rolled his chair to the door after us. With great pride, he added, "I saw General Eisenhower once. Saluted a four-star . . . at the post office." The farm boy who attended a small-town high school was on active duty not only during World War II, but also in Korea and Vietnam. His twenty-three years of service gave Merle deep satisfaction.

&&&&&

Within a minute of beginning of my interview with **Earl McKinney**, I happened to ask if he had been in the Army Air Corps. This question greatly surprised him. "Hey! You're smarter than I figured you was – to come out with that '*Army Air Corps.*' There ain't one out of thousand that knows that we did not have an Air Force during World War II, not by name. I'll be darned. I guess I have to like you a little better."

I asked Earl what he did in the Air Corps, to which he replied, "Flied them 'ere bombers." He attended gunnery school for the B-24 ("That's the one that has the two fins.") in Walla Walla, Washington. As he was on that West Coast, he assumed he would be sent to the South Pacific in the East. However, once trained on the Liberator, as the B-24 was known, he headed for the East Coast and then to England aboard a French luxury ship that was commissioned as a troop ship. "Like the Queen Mary was English, this was their big, fancy boat."

In time he flew as gunner on the B-17, the Flying Fortress. "You just pulled the trigger and pow, pow, pow, they fired, one after another." He said the fighter planes toward the end of the war did much of the firing. Still, they came under anti-aircraft fire from the ground. Near war's end, Earl's crew flew bomber missions over Berlin aboard Flying Fortress. "We flew 1000 planes, bombers, to Berlin. Did that three, four times. All came back."

Earl and I spoke of music during that era and of two musicians, especially. His favorite was Ella Mae Morse, "And this lady come by one evening to sing to the troops. Talk about luck." If Earl was impressed with my familiarity with the Army Air Corp, he would have been disappointed to know I had not heard of this once popular boogie woogie recording artist of "Cow Cow Boogie," whom he had seen in person. "Oh, I liked her music. And this is the rest of the story. "Let me lay one on ya." The girl he later married was named . . . "Ella Mae." He spoke of their courtship at a roller rink, where Earl and Ella Mae also attended boxing matches on Friday nights with her sister and her boyfriend. Like Merle's room down the hall, family photos took pride of place on the wall.

Earl was also proud of his collection of musical recordings, which included a number of gospel CDs, as well as a five-disc collection of songs from World War II. "Did you hear about Glenn Miller and World War II?" he asked quietly. Eighty years hence, I said I had but wanted to hear his take on it. "Well, he left London over the Channel and just disappeared. There's some theories. One of them is- and it's a bad one- he was in a little small plane, him and the guy that was flying the plane. The bombers, especially, sometimes you didn't find the right place to drop your bombs, you bring them back to the English Channel and dump 'em. And Miller and this guy was crossing the Channel when they were dumping." We sat in silence after he told me this hypothesis of Miller's disappearance over the English Channel, that it may have been due to returning bombers jettisoning their bombs over the Channel.

Often during our conversation, Earl circled back to his life as a boy growing up in Jefferson City. "I was born three city blocks from the Capitol building at my grandmother's house." He had a paying job from age eleven up working, oddly enough, for the 7-Up Bottling company. He and another boy put labels on the green bottles. "What they called it was 'applied color label.' Me and another boy labeled every bottle that went out of that plant. We got good at it. We could label 500 cases a day. You're not gonna believe this, I think we got five dollars a week. We worked all day on Saturday and as much as we could after school." This was big money given that there were two full-time workers in the plant who bottled and stacked from seven to five-thirty at least, most of the time a little later than that. They made two dollars a day. Actually, us, two little boys, got paid above two grown men."

He later worked for the newspaper, working his way up to printer. "At the time they issued three papers, a Sunday paper, a morning paper five days a week, and an evening paper five days a week. There was the *Post Tribune*, *Daily Capitol News* was the morning paper. I stayed there for 36 years." During his life he owned and operated several H & Bloch tax offices. He also raised cattle for 72 years. He and his wife traveled all over the Midwest to hear gospel music. "There was one guy, could sing so low. And his outfit. He was something. We probably went to five or six gospel singing every year."

"We was busy," he added in understated reflection. During our conversation, veterans home staff members came to his room to drop off laundry and to bring him meds. Both said they had missed him at breakfast and that lunch was really good that day, so to be sure to go to the cafeteria to eat. Their concern for his well-being, as well as their shared banter and teasing demonstrated their fondness for the man. I didn't want to keep him from his lunch, so we said goodbye.

He couldn't recall the exact wording, but he wanted me to see two signs that meant a great deal to him. I was not surprised to read one banner that read, **"All gave some. Some gave all."** On the opposite wall was a silhouette of a soldier and the words, **"Home of the free because of the brave."**

# VOICE TEN

## CBS AIRWAVES WORLDWIDE

## AN *IMAGINED* RADIO BROADCAST

## SEPTEMBER

## "Heart and Soul" and "McNamara's Band"

**CBS Announcer:** CBS World News now brings you a special broadcast from RAF Greenham Common just outside London. Columbia's war correspondent Walter Cronkite was on hand to experience the flight of America's stealthiest aircraft. For Mr. Cronkite's story on this silent flight, we take you to London, near the makeshift encampment in the rural English countryside from which the flight originated.

**Cronkite:** This is London. Three nights ago, on September one, from an airfield not so distant from the capital of the British Empire, one of America's bravest pilots in the Army Air Corp took to the skies over the English Channel aboard a plane with no engine, no weapons, no parachutes, and no second chances. The Waco CG-4A combat glider, dubbed the "flying coffin," is tethered by a tow rope to a Douglas C-47 Skytrain, nicknamed in the generic the Gooney Bird for its ungainly appearance. Men have further dubbed the twin aircraft, *War Wagon* and *Albatross*, respectively. The glider pilot was called Clyde [Culpepper]. Before the run, crew captains walked into the briefing room, looked at the maps and charts, and were given this night's mission. The atmosphere was like that of a school and a church. The weatherman brought us the weather, confirming the mild conditions were favorable for the assignment. The intelligence officer told us how many ack ack guns and searchlights we might expect to encounter. Then, Captain Culpepper, the wing commander, explained that a system of black and white striped markings on the underbelly of both aircraft was designed to prevent friendly fire upon the tandem flight.

The captain further advised radio silence is essential to minimize any alerting of the enemy below.

After this briefing, those flying in the C-47 went to the locker room to don parachutes and Mae Wests[1]. But the baker's dozen men of the 101st Airborne boarded the glider devoid of any such protective measures. Ejection is not an option on these powerless forays into the night skies. On similar flights, similar spacious gliders have delivered jeeps and even 75 mm Howitzers out of its front maw to the field of battle below. The brick with wings has earned it reputation as a winged wooden casket, for once cut loose by the tow plane at 500 feet above the landing area, the brave men in the cockpit know they have a mere half minute to decide where to land. There are no airstrips or runways. Furthermore, the word "land" is somewhat of a misnomer as the descent is more of a controlled crash. In addition to the planned accident, the second gravest danger for the glider, which is designed and assembled in much the same way as a boy's model airplane, is enemy anti-aircraft and machine gun fire.

The brave men who take to the skies in these giant model planes number in the hundreds, risk-tolerant mavericks attracted to the allure of an officer's pay. For them, every landing is do or die. And death is in the cards for many of these courageous aviators. Those earning an Air Medal for their valor receive a set of G-stamped wings, which the glider pilots assert stands for "Guts." For it takes an extra measure of internal fortitude to fly, much less land, a glider. Each repeated landing of these heavily laden engineless aircraft containing combat soldiers and equipment in pastures of uncharted territory behind enemy lines in total darkness is another attempt to cheat death. The minimal instrumentation with which each glider is equipped was manufactured for use in powered aircraft. Aboard an engined plane, the sensitive instruments rely on the motor's vibration to keep indicator needles from sticking. Aboard a glider, that same instrumentation relies on frequent tapping of gauges and indicators for accuracy. Once landed, if a glider happens to be undamaged, a snatch pickup is staged in which a downed glider is retrieved for reuse. Unfortunately for many of these giant bare bones transports, Rommel's asparagus–poles connected to one another and wired to explosive ordnance- wait to foil any chance of a smooth landing, especially along beachheads further fortified by armed Nazi bunkers.

Two days after a hitch-free snatch pickup of the *Wooden Wagon* and her crew, their secret operation successful, the men adjourn for an impromptu celebration. In a one-of-a-kind nightclub fashioned from the box in which the glider arrived, liquor and laughter flow freely. There's no cover charge to enter the structure they refer to as "Carnegie Hall." For it is inside the cavernous wooden crate in which the unassembled glider arrived that a makeshift officer's club was outfitted, complete with upright piano. This evening's master of ceremonies is the War Wagon's pilot Captain Culpepper himself. On the piano is the man just at the helm of the Gooney Bird responsible for delivering and retrieving the Wagon and her crew, Leo Wallace. Together the duet bangs out Hoagy Carmichael's "Heart and Soul" and give way to the Hit Parade favorite "McNamara's Band." Tired but fueled on adrenaline, coffee, cigarettes, and hooch, the men play and sing into the wee hours of the next morning.

Perhaps most interestingly, the piano, the glider, and even the G.I. coffins on hand for those for whom fate might not prove as fortunate, have a similar origin. Back home in New York City, the Steinway Piano company, forced to cease production of their glorious grands, retooled production to stay afloat. By supplying such diversified pinewood products as caskets, engineless planes, and Victory Vertical G.I. pianos for the War Department, Steinway kept its workforce, many of them women, gainfully employed throughout the war. What proved equally popular, though, were the craftsmen-constructed wooden crates in varying shapes and sizes in which the Steinway items had been shipped overseas. Tonight's nightclub is just one such example of an ingenious use to which these marvelous men and their flying machines put the shipping containers.

Following the night of song and spirits, the troop troupe return fatigued to their chosen lodging, not the Ritz Carlton but The Ritz Steinway. This shanty town of similar empty glider crates have been converted into accommodations graciously provided by the piano-cum-glider manufacturer. Used only once, and to house pre-assembled gliders at that, the sturdy packing boxcars afford more square footage per man than the regulation Quonset hut barracks allotment provided for each man at this staging ground for the Allied invasion force.

Before calling it a night, the men want to send out a hearty hello to loved ones and to those of you working for the war effort back home.

I return you now to CBS, New York.

**CBS Announcer:** You have been listening to Walter Cronkite in an eyewitness report of his experiences with the aircrew of the War Wagon and the Albatross. At 6:45pm, Eastern War Time, Mr. Cronkite will be heard again over most of these stations. This is the Columbia Broadcasting System.

[1]An inflatable lifejacket; personal flotation device used by downed aviators at sea during WWII

# AND NOW FOR THE TRUE TALE OF TOMMY TAYLOR

As a handsome dark-haired teen, Tommy Taylor made a few bucks a week as a dance instructor every Thursday night at the Frog Hop Ballroom in St. Joseph, Missouri. In the days leading up to World War II, Tommy would fox trot around the dance floor with girls who paid to take a turn around the floor with the graceful teacher who was easy on the eyes. As an instructor, Tommy was able to get into all the shows for half price. Every big-name Big Band of the day would play in venues such as the Pla-Mor in Kansas City on Saturday night and come to the Belt and Pickett to play at the Frog Hop on Mondays. As full-price admission was a buck and a quarter, Tommy not only saw but was able to rub shoulders with hit makers from the Hit Parade for half that. This is how he came to see and hear the King of Swing, Glenn Miller, and even got his autograph for 63 cents. The Glenn Miller Orchestra's hit *Chattanooga Choo Choo* was number 1 when the Japanese attacked Pearl Harbor. Due to the song's popularity, Allied air offensive rail bombings in advance of D-Day were dubbed Operation *Chattanooga Choo Choo*.

In 1942, at the peak of his career as a band leader, 38-year-old Glenn Miller decided to join the war effort. The Navy turned him down due to his age, but he persuaded the U.S. Army to accept him. Meanwhile in St. Joseph, Missouri, that same year, Tommy Taylor graduated from Lafayette High School. He, too, would be turned down by the Navy, but due to his eyesight rather than his age. Glenn Miller would later disappear in a plane over the English Channel on his way to put on a Christmas show in Paris for the troops. Months later, Tommy Taylor would likewise cross the English Channel but on an LCI, Landing Craft

Infantry, troop transport ship. His 100th birthday is March 19, 2024.

But years before, as a boy, Taylor awoke every morning to deliver the *St. Joseph Gazette* in the dark and made his rounds a second time each evening to deliver the *St. Joseph News-Press*. He did this twice daily route six days a week, with only one paper on Sundays, for five years. A gifted singer, Taylor participated in choir in high school. Although equally gifted with natural athletic ability, paper delivery didn't leave him much time outside of school hours for organized athletics at LHS. So, when he went off to college in the fall of 1942, Taylor was determined to play sports at Central College in Fayette. Not having played on a team before, when his football coach asked him what position Tommy played, without thinking the tall lanky Taylor told him right guard. Following a crushing season and bruising semester, Taylor tried out for the basketball team and rode the bench. Figuring the draft was inevitable and a career as a professional athlete not in his future, Taylor enlisted in the United States Army, reporting in February of 1943 for Fort Leavenworth.

Taylor remembers as a lowly recruit having to pick up cigarette butts. He also heard rumors that someone who was diabetic was selling his urine to others wishing to avoid service. Tommy was anxious to serve. Once processed and inducted, he and several others boarded a troop train heading south without having been told its destination. Taylor heard from a friend in the know that they were bound for Florida and the Air Corps. Arriving in St. Petersburg, most men were assigned to tents on the sand, but to Taylor's luck, he was billeted in the Albemarle

Hotel. For the Missouri boy, spending the winter months and the next 16 weeks on the beach in Florida was "hog heaven."

As a "buck private," he trained for an ordnance unit, but Tommy's luck continued when he learned of an opportunity for those who qualified based on IQ testing to attend Boston College for a fast-track engineering degree and a promotion to Second Lieutenant. Although this meant leaving the Sunshine State for a bitter Boston winter, Tommy's good fortune followed him to classes in Mechanics Hall where the Boston Symphony Orchestra also rehearsed. Here he was able to hear one of the country's greatest symphonic bands daily. During his time in Boston, he also saw Frank Sinatra perform.

Before Taylor was able to finish the Army Specialized Training Program, General Eisenhower required the attendance of all of those participating to join him in Europe on the front lines of the war. According to Tommy, Ike needed more "cannon fodder" as replacements for privates and FPCs already overseas. Thus, Taylor reported for infantry training in the woods of Virginia at Camp Pickett. Here the 78th Infantry Lightning Division received rifle and pistol training at a shooting range so well used, the trees behind the targets were sheared off from the constant barrage of bullet fire. Taylor qualified as a sharpshooter on the M-1 rifle and as an expert with the .45 caliber pistol. As the side arm would be the gun he would carry, Taylor was content with this designation.

He returned to ordnance training and became a 60 mm mortar gunner in a five-man squad that also consisted of a "head honcho" sergeant, an assistant gunner, and two ammunition bearers. He earned his PFC stripe just as everyone else tapped to go overseas automatically made PFC without going through the requisite training. This promotion from private came with a raise in pay to $21 monthly. On pay day, Taylor remembers fierce gambling among guys whose entire forearms were loaded with the wrist watches they won off suckers playing craps.

Their rush to readiness ended with a trip over the Atlantic to Bournemouth, England. A month after arriving in Southampton, the Lightning Division changed ships, boarding an LCI, Landing Craft Infantry, ship by sliding down a tube from the taller ship to the smaller transport. Crossing the English Channel to Le Havre, Taylor took note of untold numbers of sunken ship masts sticking out of the water in the aftermath of the Normandy invasion. From France, the 78th were trucked north to Belgium.

On the front line, Taylor was confronted with the choice of firing mortar or machine guns at the enemy. As firing light artillery in defilade meant not shooting directly at those shooting directly at you but rather from the protection behind a berm, Taylor opted for mortar. His company reported as replacements for previous soldiers who had dug foxholes before being shipped out. These foxholes were a few feet deep and covered by logs covered by dirt covered by rain gear to keep dry. Considered cozy and safe, men entered through a small opening and stayed warm inside their "fart sacks," as their sleeping bags were called. One night during shelling, a piece of shrapnel landed on Taylor's fart sack. Instinctively he grabbed the red-hot smoldering metal and tossed it off.

Life in a foxhole in Aachen, Germany wasn't as luxurious as his earlier stay at the Hotel Albemarle in Florida. Taylor and the guys in his foxhole constructed a stove out of a round one pound coffee tin filled with dirt and kerosene for warmth. This makeshift camp stove caught fire in the middle of the night, charring their faces with soot and sending a signal to the Germans of their whereabouts. Next, they improved on their design by using an empty shell casing with a smokestack fabricated from cardboard.

Every night for a month, a German light aircraft flew over their position, earning the name "Bed Check Charlie" from the men. By day Taylor stood sentry with an M-1 he found and found to be safer than the inaccurate sights of his pistol. During this time, the troops also experienced buzz bombs and learned to hit the deck when the buzzing stopped, for a detonation was imminent.

After a month, the company received orders to "push off." They were ordered to remain quiet so as not to alert the enemy of their advance. The tanks, however, by the hundreds rumbled loud enough to announce their approach. During this trek, men billeted in houses abandoned due to the barrage of bombing in the area. One day, Taylor crossed a fence and found himself in a snow-covered minefield. His assistant gunner yelled for him to get out of there, so Taylor retraced his snowy footprints. He later learned this was not the thing to do, as it increased the likelihood of detonation when the snowpack released the trigger of the landmine. Fortunately, this did not happen, and Taylor was able to retreat without incident.

One night on guard duty Taylor heard the crackle of leaves under foot. Having been trained to give the command to halt three times and then shoot, Taylor yelled, "Halt!" The rustle of leaves continued. Taylor gave the command to halt a second time. The sounds continued. A third time he yelled, "Halt!" Just as Taylor prepared to fire, a dog came into sight. Greatly relieved, he lowered his rifle.

Some might say Taylor's luck ran out shortly after he took shrapnel in his arm during a battle. Tommy Taylor says he was one of the lucky ones. He sustained a compound complete fracture to the ulna and was transported to Brussels by truck. From there he was operated on and sent on to Glasgow, Scotland. He boarded the Queen Mary as one of 15,000 passengers returning to the States. Due to the number of passengers, the ship's ballast had been removed and it teetered precariously throughout the trip home. Taylor says he painted the deck green from seasickness as the ship zigged and zagged across the Atlantic to avoid German U-boats. He recalls seeing the moon in the night sky at a distance in one direction, and then again from another direction later in the evening.

Two uniformed officers arrived at his house to speak with his parents, who were understandably alarmed by their appearance. They reported that Tommy had been "slightly wounded" and was on his way home. Six months later, after a recuperative stint in a hospital in Denver, Tommy was issued $35 and mustered out of the Army. Wearing the "ruptured duck," the gold pin worn by the honorably discharged servicemen so that folks knew they were in uniform but in transit rather than AWOL, he thumbed a ride with someone traveling across the country to his home in St. Joseph, Missouri. Tommy often hitchhiked, including one winter when stranded in freezing weather, he stayed the night at the Roxy Theater in New Franklin, Missouri. He sought refuge from the snow but could hardly sleep for the cramped folding theater chair and the sound of rats eating popcorn on the movie house floor.

Tommy availed himself of the G.I. Bill to attend the University of Missouri for a bachelor's degree and then attended UMKC for dentistry school. He started a dental practice and married a "cute little cheerleader." He took up singing lead in a series of barbershop quartets that won numerous state championships and even qualified for international competition. Along with a bass, a tenor, and a baritone, Tommy Taylor took "That Old Black Magic," "Yes, Indeed," and "Easy Street" to many contests and returned with many a trophy. Dr. Taylor retired after practicing dentistry for 35 years. He credits Carol Sue, good fortune, and a fitness regimen that includes running a marathon 50 years ago at age 50 for his longevity.

### VIGNETTE AND VOICE ELEVEN
### OCTOBER 1975
### "House of the Rising Sun," "Can the Circle Be Unbroken," "Leaning on The Everlasting Arms," and "Lili Marlene"

Unlike most thieves, Jilly later reflected, this one knocked on the door. No one had observed his journey up the long, graveled drive, guitar case knocking his knee with every long stride. A car they would have heard that quiet Saturday morning in October, but he didn't have a car. All he owned was contained within the guitar case and the army green duffle he carried.

Traveling salesmen were rare at this isolated farmhouse miles from an isolated tiny town in this isolated southwest Mississippi backwater. Even that town's name, Zion, ranked it as the last, and least, of Mississippi's settlements. Still, her mom occasionally waved away the odd salesman who wandered into their orbit. Unless he was selling encyclopedias.

Her folks had a weakness for *The World Book*, books of any sort really, a weakness they passed to their children. The Elliots might not have food for dinner the night before or for breakfast following morning, but during the wait for the next day's free school lunch, the Elliots had a sampling of alphabetic tomes devoted to a scattering of consonants, assorted vowels, and the occasional annual supplement to pour over night after night. "A platypus!" eight-year-old John would say, fascinated, from behind the P volume.

"A blowfish?" Kent, at eleven, was skeptical. These wonders seemed as unreal as the fairy stories they read, but there they were in *The World Book* encyclopedia so they must be true. Faye looked up from the 1973 Yearbook edition at a sound from the porch.

The young man who startled them with his knock would startle them further when the door opened to his rangy frame. He was tall, over six feet, clad in a navy denim snap-front shirt, Wrangler jeans, and cowboy boots. None of that was unusual. It was his face. That deeply tanned face, with its prominent nose, high forehead, and lake green eyes, was immediately recognizable as their father's, a precise rendition of Ray Elliots at 25.

"I'm your son," was hardly necessary, but he'd clearly waited many years to say it. "Dean." The significance of this announcement was intended for their father. The youngest of Dean's half-siblings crowded in to stare. Reggie, the oldest of the traveler's six heretofore unbeknownst siblings, led his fiancé from the room.

"You kids go upstairs," Ida, their mother, said. She surely knew they crouched hidden on the steps, barely breathing, as Ida followed Ray and his son into the living room, empty now but for books of knowledge left scattered about.

From under the stairwell the children heard their mother, Ida, say, "You'll stay with us." Ray remained silent, immobile, as Ida struggled to fill the silence. Finally, she said, "Let's get you settled in with the boys."

The old painted white farmhouse was typical of its day. The main floor consisted of a modest kitchen, a dining room with mix-matched chairs to seat a family of eight, the lone bathroom, a living area, and Ray and Ida's bedroom situated nearest the old wood stove. The stairs led from the living room, rising straight to a bedroom to the left and another to the right. Each of the gabled wooden bedrooms contained three twin beds. In the girls' bedroom, Faye, the bossiest of the trio, had chosen the bed near the window. Sue, the practical one, occupied the middle, and Jilly, the littlest and most imaginative, had the bed nearest the doorless frame.

"Where is he going to sleep?" Sue whispered. With Reggie home on leave from the Army for his wedding, the boys' bedroom was at capacity. Dean quickly learned he would be occupying a pallet on the floor. He would bunk with the boys and have a bed when the newlyweds returned to base.

Over the coming days, weeks, and months, the children gleaned from overheard conversations that they were, in fact, the third of Ray Elliot's families. Three older sisters lived with their mother in Germany, and this young man, Ray Dean as their father called him, and his sister Brenda were from Tupelo.

Even as young children, none of this came as a great surprise to the Elliot kids. Their father had insisted his oldest daughter in this third iteration of Ray's family be named Raymona Faye. So, of course, he would have insisted his first son be named for him as well. In coming years, they would discover that the three additional sisters, the eldest daughters of his eleven offspring, were named Marlene, Eleanor, and Dorinda, the latter two being twins. They would also learn the three girls born in Allied Occupied Germany following war's end had been christened with appellations that happened to mirror those of a triad of their father's antebellum dalliances.

But despite their father's prolific past, the entire family were enthralled with their new older brother. All except Reggie, the mentor to the current clan, who married his bride and hastily departed with her for his base in Little Rock. The littler kids recovered from Reggie's absence, consoled by the arrival of Ray Dean, as their father decreed he be called, and, like devoted puppies, followed him around the farm they sharecropped.

Within days, Ray Dean snapped open his case to withdraw a used acoustic guitar to accompany Ray, who played by ear at their ugly green piano for family singalongs. The younger boys kept the beat on makeshift kitchen pots and pans for drums, and the girls kept time with cutlery. Even Ida would join in their songfest and lend her Ozark contralto to the mix.

Nights were sultry in the low-lying Mississippi delta, and Ray and Ray Dean would sit on the porch after everyone had gone to bed and continue to play music with but one battered six string between them. Father would teach son Hank Williams chords on the guitar, and then they would swap, and son would teach father Bob Dylan riffs.

One July night the younger kids drifted off to sleep to the duo playing a version of "House of the Rising Sun," unlike any they had heard on the AM radio. Both seemed to know the song, so Jilly wasn't sure who was picking. But no sooner had she fallen asleep than Jilly awoke from a nightmare and couldn't get back to sleep, the humidity and heat were so oppressive.

She crept to the screened window without waking her sisters to listen to the music coming from the porch below. They were singing "Can the Circle Be Unbroken," a hymn often played during what her father called their Elliot Family Hootenanny.

After the evening's swan song, there was silence but for the chorus of cicadas and katydids which continued from beyond the tree line. Jilly listened for the screen to bang shut, the impromptu concert over. As she waited, she began to doze at the window. She fell back into her dream but reawakened with a start to realize they were still out there in the night, talking about a song called "Lili Marlene." Jilly heard her dad say it was the prettiest song ever written, one that could make grown men cry.

The murmur of the men's low voices gave her comfort, so she strained to hear. Ray Dean said he couldn't help but notice the green piano, that he'd seen one of those before in a place he called Tie-Land. That ugly piano had followed Jilly's family everywhere. Her father explained how he and three buddies had picked it up at an auction for $10. Literally, picked the thing up and loaded it on a flatbed truck. The Elliots had moved "Tank," as the kids dubbed it, seven times before it landed in the house in which they currently resided.

"That ain't just any ol' piano, it's Steinway," Ray concluded. But as her father relayed the instrument's pedigree, Jilly imagined this place, Tie-Land, that Ray Dean had mentioned. All the men wore ties. Some, like her principal, wore bow ties. Others wore regular skinny black ties, like their preacherman, Reverend Lancaster. Some even wore bolos, the string ties her father favored, his favorite being one with rattlesnake rattles affixed by silver filigree to the ends.

A funny word that Ray Dean kept repeating for her father caught her attention, so she leaned against the screen to hear better. "Davika, it means 'Little Goddess,'" Ray Dean said. "Her momma picked it."
Her dad allowed as he always picked the names. "That reminds me, your sister, the one you call 'Brenda,' her name's really 'Dorinda.' That's the name I give her. Your mom musta gone and changed it." In fact, Ray allowed as how he had a few girls in Munich, and "the second one's Dorinda, too." Ray Dean made a joke about Ray's past where names, and the children attached to them were concerned. Jilly froze, fearing her father's wrath at this cavalier comment.

Instead, Ray just laughed and said, "You got a point there, boy." Then he continued, "Nah, it was just easier thata way. I loved her mor'n I ever loved any one person, but I didn't have the money to bring her over, much less her and the girls. Them kids woulda had nothin but trouble here in the States. Not ever' one's as taken by the frauleins, especially 'round these parts. 'Course they was in for a hard time there, too, bein' half-Amerikaner, but at least they was in their own country. We wrote for a while, but I didn't speak mucha her talk, and she didn't have much English. No, I just made up my mind to make a clean break. Had my momma write to Lili Marlene, that weren't her real name but I couldn't put my tongue around what they called her over there. Said to tell her I's dead. Said, make somethin' up. She wrote 'n said I was kilt in a tornado, in New Mexico of all things," at this Ray let out a laugh. "I said, 'Damn, Momma, that's layin' it on thick. I wonder about my Lili Marlene sometimes, how she's gettin' along." Ray Dean gave a mirthless laugh. Pretty soon, Jilly heard the screen door bang shut.

For a time, Ray Dean seemed earnest in his desire to please their father. On the first Sunday it was apparent Ray Dean had never entered a house of worship. He stood awkwardly when everyone stood and sat when they sat, but always a beat or two behind the others. "Ray Dean plays guitar. How about if he plays with the organ and piano?" Ray asked the preacher. The pastor squirmed at this most unorthodox suggestion, but relented, Ray having previously run sideways with the preacher on sundry matters.

Within weeks "Leaning on the Everlasting Arms" developed a markedly hillbilly twang, the organist and pianist stepping up the tempo. Unless you listened closely to the words "Are you washed (pronounced worshed) in the Blood, in the soul cleansing blood of the lamb," the song might have sounded like a Scott Joplin tune. Church, for a time at least, became something the Elliots and the more spirited members of the congregation looked forward to, although Reverend Lancaster wondered if this wasn't somewhat a sacrilege for their song service to sound like a honkytonk.

Summer gave way to fall, which conceded to winter. Besides being an itinerant farmer, Ray worked in construction, a seasonal trade. The family might feast in the summer when there was work but often fasted through the cold winter months when jobs were scarce.

"What's for breakfast?" little brother John would say hopefully, but even he knew that, unless his dad had made their mother apply for assistance from the county again, it would be water gravy with water biscuits morning, noon, and night. If there was little money for groceries, there was even less for gift giving come Christmas. Even had Ray the money, he wasn't inclined toward layaways, to speak nothing of his suspicion with banks with their Christmas club savings accounts. So, when their now next-to-oldest brother, proudly uniformed, and his quite unexpectedly expectant bride visited for Christmas that year bearing bounteous gifts for the children who had rarely celebrated the holiday with presents, the Elliot children were elated. To children unaccustomed to receiving presents, ribbons and bows and their contents were novelties beyond imagining. Faye, Sue, and Jilly each received precious stones, for Sue a golden necklace with a tiny ruby, for Faye a garnet, and for Jilly a silver chain with a diamond - a diamond! Jilly would never forget the pride on Reggie's face as she and her sisters opened his gifts. She imagined he would not soon forget the looks on his little sisters' as they gaped in astonishment at such sparkling treasures.

Not to be outdone by the usurper whose bed he had usurped, Ray Dean had elemental gifts of his own. For the boys, he had carved walnut slingshots, the composition and the ammo being from the same tree, he joked. For the girls, he gave arrowheads he had found in the creek bed.

The end of the holiday break had always meant heading back to school to hear stories of Santa's bounty. "What did you get for Christmas?" is a despised question for children who receive nothing. In solidarity, the children adhered to their standard deflection, "Oh, you know, stuff. What did you get?" That January, however, they may have worn the same hand-me-down clothes on their first day back to school, but they also sported delicate, glowing necklaces polished every night before the girls carefully consigned the jewelry to their royal blue velvet boxes, lined in triplicate on the windowsill.

Oddly, Jilly did not recall that Ray Dean ever worked during those months he lived with them, except in Dad's presence. They lived miles from civilization, and he had no car. The siblings never resented Ray Dean's going missing as they fed pigs and plucked chickens and chopped wood for the stove. No one told Dad that their oldest brother was usually sitting with his back to a tree, chewing a toothpick and gazing ruminatively into the distance, as the others chored.

What the children really wanted was more information, details about these other unspoken branches on their family tree. Sisters in Germany? Were they still living there, or had their father brought his family home with him when he was transferred back to the States after the Occupation? Had their mother known? Had her father, their Grandpa Adamson, realized that Dad had been married twice before he married Mom when she was still a teenager? The questions remained unasked. The children feared violent reproof had they been voiced.

What they learned that spring was that Ray Dean was even more like their drifter father than they knew. They woke one cold April morning to find that he'd gone. Broken-hearted as they were that he hadn't said goodbye, that feeling grew as they realized the few valuables they possessed were gone with him. Maybe he felt they owed him for the loss of his father all those years.

Jilly wondered how much the pawnbroker, whose three golden balls were the symbol of St. Nicholas, gave him for those three tiny necklaces.

## VIGNETTE TWELVE

## NOVEMBER 1968

### "Chopsticks"

Every year Frances and her mother Margot always drove the sixteen hours north to Minot to visit Margot's mother and dad over three days rather than two. It could have easily been done in two, but Andy, Margot's husband and Frances's dad didn't want Margot to wear herself out. So, they planned for her and the girl to lay over in Wisconsin and again in Minnesota to stay at a roadside motel. They would eat pancakes at a Howard Johnson and make a big time of it. Andy always had to work, so it was just the two girls taking to the open road in a Ford coupe.

They didn't always stay in the same lodging, but one side trip was a constant. Every summer, they made it a point to stop in Wisconsin to purchase a new American flag. Andy's sister Annabeth's husband had worked for Eder Flag for years, and since Margot's father had faithfully displayed the stars and stripes from the time they only had 48 stars, she purchased a replacement for the faded and windblown one from her brother-in-law in time for Flag Day every year.

Frances was the joy of Margot and Andy's life, arriving as she had late in their married life. When others their age were raising teenagers, Margot discovered she was expecting. Despite persistent health issues, she carried the baby girl to term, and the couple doted on their blue-eyed princess daily.

On this particular trip back home to the Jacobson homestead, as they had extra time, Margot stopped at the Wisconsin State Fair in Milwaukee so the girl could experience candy floss. Frances asked if she could have a funnel cake as well. She drew the line, however, at letting Frances climb the greased pole with a twenty-dollar bill at the top and participating in the greased pig contest. What was it about grease and state fairs? One year they took a whole week and detoured hundreds of miles through South Dakota for a free glass of ice water at Wall Drug, to visit the Mitchell Corn Palace, and to climb around Mount Rushmore.

Unlike Margot, Frances was athletic and somewhat of a tomboy, preferring to be outside any day to staying inside and practicing piano. In that regard, Frances reminded Margot of the girl's namesake and uncle. Except Francis loved to play the piano and was self-taught. Never had a lesson in his life but could hear something once and play it by ear. The only song Margot ever felt confident playing, even after years of lessons, was "Chopsticks," which her beloved Francis taught her.

He used to give his little sister Margot piggyback rides long after she should have outgrown them and led her on a pony around the barn. She still had the tiny tea set he sent her one Christmas when he went away and would give it to Frances one day. She would tell her about him one day. But for now, she needed to prepare herself for this year's homecoming. As they crossed the prairie and approached the century-old family wheat farm that sat on the confluence of the Souris River and a lesser-known Mouse tributary, she imagined her folks would see their approach as they passed over the coulee.

The last couple of summers, Margot had returned between planting and harvest with trepidation. Her father was beginning to act completely out of character and had grown increasingly vocal about Communists, a fear she thought unfounded, in Minot. She feared he might be suffering from the onset of dementia after she witnessed him yell at a boy delivering a weekly shopper to come back and take his propaganda with him.

Late one lucid summer day, however, a cub reporter and a photographer were sent to the farm to snap a picture of Jacobsen taking down the flag as he had done every evening for over thirty years. His neighbor Tollefson had mentioned it at coffee at a table full of townsfolk. The men were traveling the countryside looking for patriotic images as the Vietnam war raged on. Jacobsen didn't speak a word to the reporter, but he had not run the journalists off. A photograph of him raising the country's colors ran in black and white on the front page that Fourth of July. Mother, never talkative in the best of times, also declined to speak to the newspaper men. Mother hardly even spoke during her daughter and granddaughter's yearly visit, but the girls could usually pry some small details about the weather, the garden, and the bird migrations.

Frances would remember this trip for the discovery she made. In the makeshift basement bedroom her grandmother always made up for them, there hung a dark maroon curtain over a small alcove closet by the furnace. Rooting around in the closet, she discovered a small wooden chest about the size of a shoe box. Margot came downstairs to check on the girl, who ordinarily would have been outside running around "like a wild Indian," as folks in the Dakotas were wont to say. Margot thought favorably of this racially charged idiom and envied indigenous children if they were free to play outside.

"Look at this cool stuff, Mom. Whose is it?" she asked when Margot found her. Margot took the box and put it on the bed. She lifted each item out one by one, turning them over and laying them gently on the bed. A felt Minot Magi high school pennant, a raccoon tail, a feather, a pocketknife, a harmonica, a rattlesnake rattle, a pocket watch, a thin, dried leather wallet with stitching around the edges that contained a YMCA id card on which "Francis Jacobsen" was faintly typed, and certificate for flying lessons. A smaller box contained a medal with George Washington in profile on a purple ribbon.

With each article, Frances heard stories about Margot's brother, the one closest to her mother in age. Frank played baseball in high school. He hunted critters with a .22. He could pick up and play any instrument or sing any song without ever having taken a lesson. He swam at the YMCA with friends. (Swimsuits were not allowed, but it only occurred to her in hindsight to question this policy.) He had taken flying lessons, much to Mother's dismay (It gave her "a bad feeling," as many things did) but had stopped after Karl told him to have sense enough either to quit flying lessons altogether or to stop writing home about it. The existence of the certificate revealed he had opted for the latter. And he died on the Solomon Islands saving men even younger than he was and over whom he was in charge. His death was deemed a casualty of war by an errant shell launched from a U.S. gun boat.

Margot vowed the girl to secrecy, telling her not to mention the box or its contents to her grandparents. Each year when they returned, the mother and daughter reopened the box, and a little bit of Frank seemed to come into being for both of them with each item's retelling.

## VOICE TWELVE

## NORTH DAKOTA, NOVEMBER 1944

## "You're a Grand Old Flag," "I'll Dance at Your Wedding," "Kiss Me Goodnight, Sergeant Major"

Jacobsen only left his 160-wheat farm that November day in 1943 because the missus needed some Vicks VapoRub for their daughter, who had been born sickly fifteen years earlier. His four boys had been hale and healthy from birth and were now spread to the four winds, serving their country overseas. Karl, the oldest, was in the Army. The twins, Ralph and Richard, were in the Air Corp. Karl, who had served a tour in Europe and was now in the South Seas, encouraged their youngest brother, Frank, the last to be called up, to join the Navy. Karl had seen men and boys die daily and thought it better to live in a tropical paradise than die in a cold, muddy wasteland.

Frank compromised and signed with the Marines, which wasn't at all what Karl had in mind. Their old man, having himself experienced trench fighting in the Great War, was proud his sons were doing their part but would never say as much. Just as he never told them he loved them, or his wife, whom he called Mother, for that matter.

Jacobsen was at the chemists picking up the salve when his neighbor, Tollefson, approached him and asked could they have a word outside. Tollefson's nephew delivered telegrams for Western Union and had asked his uncle for a ride out to the Jacobsen place, it being too great a distance to ride his Schwinn. Tollefson had said he would just take the cable on the return trip, but now here was Jacobsen in the flesh.

Jacobsen set the Vicks on the counter and followed Tollefson outside. Those inside the drug store saw the two men exchange words and an envelope exchange hands. Coincidentally, onlookers knew that two out-of-place-looking men in sailor suits had been looking for someone. To their knowledge, though, none of the Jacobson boys were Navy.

Jacobsen, in heavy canvas chore coat, received whatever word Tollefson had to say, accepted his envelope, and walked to the Dodge truck. Seemingly having forgotten all about the mentholated chest rub, Jacobsen drove off. Tollefson crossed the street to the diner, entered, delivered whatever message he was sent to carry, and returned to the pharmacy. He drew a bill from the wallet in the bib of his overalls and paid for the Vicks VapoRub.

Within minutes, the pair of officials in smart white pants that were entirely impractical for November North Dakota came out of the diner and left in a black Buick. Jacobsen was two blocks ahead of them, parked in front of St. Leo's where he told Tollefson to have them meet him. The farmer had gone in the side door of the church offices to find Father Rex. Seeing Jacobsen's truck parked out front, the officers sidestepped snow and marched up the sidewalk and entered the vestibule. They took off their white caps with black patent leather visors as their eyes adjusted to the dim interior.

Neighbors living next door to the rectory say that moments later, Father Rex got into the church Plymouth and followed the truck out to the Jacobsen place, followed by the black Buick.

Mother was hanging clothes on the line when she saw dust rising over the coulee. From a distance, she saw her husband's truck, followed by a Plymouth she recognized as being Father Rex, and an unfamiliar black Buick. Behind them came the rusty red Ford belonging to their neighbor, Tollefson. The same wind that swept across the prairie to dry her family's clothes and turn the windmill that pumped their water often blew in an ill omen. This gave her a bad feeling.

From inside the house, Margot watched the five of them, her dad, Father Rex, two men in white short sleeves, and her friend

Annabeth's father, Mr. Tollefson, get out of their vehicles and walk toward Mother. They all proceeded up the cracked sidewalk to the house. From inside, Margot's racing heart led to wheezing. She heard six sets of feet ascend the wooden porch steps, open the screen and heavy wooden door, and enter the front room. Though she tried not to, she began to cough.

Mr. Tollefson came to her where she sat covered in a quilt on the davenport and handed her a short cobalt blue jar. "Here you go, sister," he said. Margot was bewildered by this but accepted the mentholated ointment. She noted his kind blue eyes, the same eyes Annabeth and her brother Andy had. She was sweet on Andy, the fact of which she had sworn Annabeth to secrecy.

Although no one told Margot anything, the concern for her heart and lungs being great, she surmised that one of her brothers had died. She knew better than to ask. So many subjects were off limits in their home, and subject to Mother especially having a "bad feeling about." Margot was left to wonder and greatly feared who it might be but felt bad about wishing it were anyone but Frank. With time, she intuited it had to be Frank, but no one said as much to her. It was more by omission, as his name was never once mentioned by either parent and there was no service. It took months for her to reach a definitive conclusion. And in late summer the twins came home, the war having ended. By fall, Karl returned, so she knew she was right; it was Frank. Francis Bernard Jacobsen, her favorite brother, the one who pounded by ear on the parlor piano and sang George M. Cohan's star-spangled "You're a Grand Old Flag" at the top of his healthy lungs.

The day after Karl's return, from her place on the davenport, she overheard the three remaining brothers talking amongst themselves. "I'll Dance at Your Wedding" was usually one of her favorite songs because Frank banged it out on the now-silent piano. Now it blared from the radio in the kitchen but brought her no joy. Their parents gone to mass at St. Leo's, Karl turned the radio up even louder, intentionally she thought, and repeated what he had been told by someone on the Solomon Islands. She willed her heart to slow and her breathing to quieten so she could hear his words over the music.

As it was, she picked up words and pieces between lyrics. *Frank rushed up a steep incline.* "I'll drink to your father." *Bougainville. Orders to get high as possible.* "I'll drink to your mother." *Dig fox holes. Barricade.* "Then I'll have another for Auld Lang Syne." *Prepare to rush over the cliff after shelling from the American boats. Shelling came earlier than expected.* "Save some of that rice they throw." *Frank grabbed two men, threw them into the hole.* "Drink to me father." *Shielded them with his body.* "Drink to me mother." *Friendly fire.*

The song ended. Margot wondered at this expression, *friendly fire*. It seemed like an oxymoron, a word she had learned in school on one of the days she had been well enough to attend. Did this mean that Frank died at the hands of his own side? She couldn't determine if this made his death better for not having been killed by someone meaning for him to die, or worse for the utter random senselessness. The latter she decided.

Other than that brief conversation, punctuated as it was by song, she only ever heard Frank's name mentioned once again in their home. Karl told the visiting Tollefsons that Frank had been buried in Manila, but not in the presence of Mother or their father. Karl said by all accounts Frank was admired and loved by his men. He'd even heard that Frank used to play one of the blue gray pianos for them. Two had actually been dropped from the air, one a spare in case the other didn't survive the landing. One man in Frank's company had written to Karl that his brother frequently received requests for "Kiss Me Goodnight, Sergeant Major." That was the last time Margot heard anyone in her family mention their youngest son. Each in his or her own way grieved his loss in silence. But with each new day, Jacobsen flew a flag from the porch pillar and brought it in every night.

\*\*\*

# A BRIEF HISTORY OF THE BATTLE OF THE BULGE

The Battle of the Bulge was the second time Hitler sent Panzer tanks through the Ardennes Forest. Earlier, in May 1940 German high command had come up with an audacious plan to cut through the hilly, dense forest with armored divisions on the way to the English Channel. At the time merely evil and tyrannical and not the drug-addled, paranoid despot he would later become, Hitler disagreed with this tactic as being too risky. He planned instead to invade France and arrive at the Channel from the north through Holland and the Low Countries.

However, before that plan could be enacted, a German plane carrying a secret message to that effect crash landed in Belgium. The classified plans fell into Allied hands. Furious that his strategy was no longer top secret, Hitler decided to do both– —go ahead as a rouse on a limited scale as planned with the Northern route invasion to throw the Allies off track but also send the bulk of Germany's armored divisions with air support through the Ardennes as a Blitzkrieg sneak attack. This overwhelming show of force created panic as German panzers plowed through the Ardennes, demoralizing the Allies. What took Germany five years during WW I only took five days. By catching the Allies off guard, Germany was able to swiftly move to the Channel.

In an entirely different scenario, four years later, following D-Day and the liberation of Paris and at a time when half of Germany's army was under siege in Stalingrad on the Eastern front during a Russian winter, a deranged but emboldened Hitler, decided against all reason to set his sights on the harbor at Antwerp to the West. Having survived a bombing assassination attempt from within his own Reich high command, a galvanized completely delusional Hitler goes against the largely unspoken consensus of generals who fear being seen as disloyal by voicing opposition based on reason. Herr Hitler boldly sends Panzers once again through the Ardennes, counting this time on winter weather and the element of surprise as being on his side.

Amidst freezing fog and mud, columns of German tanks do take the Allies by surprise and create a bulge. Encouraged to surrender, General McAuliffe refused, issuing his one-word response, "Nuts." And the weather, doing what weather does best, changes. This change in forecast resulted in a turning of the tide of the battle. The fog lifted and the conditions allowed for 101st Airborne reinforcements. Patton's Army lived to fight another day. Essential supplies and ammunition were even delivered by wooden gliders, which Steinway produced, along with coffins and Vertical Victory Government Issue pianos, during the war.

Victory Verticals were known to have been air dropped and even played still cocooned within their protective crates along the front lines of battle fields to entertain troops. Many were delivered to hospitals to calm wounded soldiers. But pianos are merely inanimate musical instruments with 88 keys. Impromptu singalongs and scheduled U.S.O. entertainment relied on those whose hands could play instruments. Accompanying the voices of G.I.s lifted in song, to achieve their aim, the troops at a keyboard helped boost morale and reminded troops what they were fighting for, home.

As for what has become known as the Battle of the Bulge, outnumbered by an Allied front fortified with Sherman tanks and air drops of much needed reinforcement, the depleted army of the Third Reich was essentially left to limp home during the coldest winter on record. Despite heavy casualties, the Allies held the line and rebuffed this second German invasion. Hitler and those close to him retreated to his bunker, never to leave.

### HENRI'S STORY

As a tour guide in Bastogne, Henri Mignon recounts these anecdotes regarding his experience as a boy living in Belgium during the Battle of the Bulge. As you read his words, presented in English (not his native language), imagine his very thick accent. Thank you to Becky Harrold for sharing her videos of Henri speaking during a recent tour of WWII sites.

"I remember the day of the German attack. I was nine. I had a brother who was eleven. We went to school. A teacher was standing in the front of the school. He said, 'Don't be scared. Return home. You can come back later. Yes, we came back. One year later. It was the longest holiday of my life. After the battle we had a long holiday, and you know it was a dream for the boys, all the wreckage was still there, and we were continually playing on tanks and airplanes. Next September, very bad news, back to school! We couldn't believe it. We lost our liberty. We had an additional day out because the mine experts came to clean the battlefield. We showed them where the grenades and shells were."

"When we returned home, Germans were there. They always arrived in the sidecar. Like in the movie. We progressively became completely occupied. When I say completely, we had Germans from the kitchen to the attic. They had taken all the beds. We slept on the floor, side by side with the German soldiers. They were covered with lice. Consequently, we were covered with lice. We went to the American aid station at the church. Covered with DDT, completely white. But the lice came back. We put our clothes in the oven."

"Beginning of the battle we were to some extent lucky because were occupied by a detachment of the German Wehrmacht (regular army). My mother was obliged to cook for them. We received part of the food. A bit later we were joined by another detachment. These SS Germans were completely different. Black uniform, very excited, young, arrogant, cruel. It was an army inside the army. They were even hated by the other Germans. One SS division had burned 600 people in a church. It was the Panzer SS division."

"We could see groups of hundreds of bombers, B17s and B24s, flying to bomb the German towns. I don't know if you can imagine what it is to see hundreds of bombers. Hundreds of bombers during the day. At night it was the British Royal Air Force, better equipped for night. Flying in the opposite direction we had the German V-1s, the buzz bombs. We would say a drone today flying to bomb British towns. I remember the first one, it was flying very loud with the terrible noise. Once you have heard a V-1 in your life you will never forget it. It was a pulse jet. And we very quickly learned it was dangerous when the engine stopped. It was a sign it was going to crash. It was terrifying. The first liberation, September 44, easy operation for the Allied troops because the

Germans were fleeing. We spent hours and hours cheering young American soldiers. They were dropping chocolate, chewing gum, biscuits, which were absolutely horrid, cigarettes." (Henri noted that American Wonder bread was the softest he's ever known.)

"When I was a boy I have seen almost excessively American soldiers. When we went back to school, we had a job after school. We visited our American friends because they wanted to exchange their Russian eggs and potatoes and it was our job to purchase for the American soldiers. And I had always an additional request— they wanted to have cognac, a reminder from Normandy, and they always had a question: 'Do you have a great (meaning older or big) sister? They were very interested in our sisters!"

*Henri's father died on the last day of the battle, blown up by an artillery shell when he was out collecting snow to heat for water.

# VIGNETTE THIRTEEN

## DECEMBER

### 1946, 1996
### "Thanks for the Memory"

Every night in the months since returning from the war, J.L. unloaded his pants pockets as he did at the end of each day and placed his keys, change, and billfold on the bureau. He didn't think of himself as the sentimental sort, but he had hung on to two letters in the last year. One from Harry Truman, and that last one from Jeannie.

He picked up the wallet and removed the folded envelope he had carried with him throughout Europe, out of habit more than anything, since the day he received it. The inked return address was entirely faded, but the fragile onionskin letter inside was still intact. He didn't re-read it. He knew its contents by heart. It was the only remaining contact he had with her, as he had burned her bundled letters at her request somewhere in the Ardennes. This one he had hung onto for the return address, but the only record he had of her newly married name and place of residence had entirely worn away.

Tonight, he had stopped by the bar with a few guys from work for a beer. Then he stayed for another one. Someone played that song he had seen in a picture show with Jeannie. Then he heard Bob Hope sing it during a U.S.O. performance accompanied by a blonde on a little green piano. Tonight, when someone put a nickel in the jukebox and played it, he knew it was time to go home. Still, it sang on in his head, "Thanks for the memory . . . Letters with sweet little secrets

That couldn't be put in a day wire . . . Too bad it all had to go haywire.

That's life, I guess . . . Thanks for the memory . . . Of faults that you

forgave . . . Thanks for the memory."

He folded his pants over the chair and hung his shirt on a nail and tried to stop the song. "We said goodbye with a highball . . . And I got as high as a steeple . . . But we were intelligent people . . . No tears, no fuss, hooray for us . . . Strictly entre nous, darling, how are you?

. . . And how are all those little dreams that never did come true?

Awfully glad I met you, cheerio, tootle-oo."

He had dropped the envelope, letter still inside, in the trash, turned off the lamp, and turned in for the night. He tried to put her out of his mind for the next fifty years.

In time he met a nice girl. She had a daughter. Her husband had not had the same good fortune to return from the war. She and J.L. married and had a nice life. He became a second father to her. When she passed away, he thought that was it for love. But then he received a letter. The handwriting was so familiar.

She said she had seen in an alumni bulletin that his wife had passed and wished to share her condolences. Would he be attending the class reunion in the spring?

He did not reply to her letter. But on the night of the alumni banquet, J.L. put on some Old Spice. He didn't want to admit to himself that he was keeping an eye out for her. He almost didn't recognize Jeannie. She was no longer brunette. Her hair had gone completely white. But she was more gorgeous than ever. Despite that he was completely bald, she knew him at once and asked if the seat next to him was taken. It was not.

Somehow, they realized the essence of time and spoke as if the intervening years had been but a moment. They skipped any small talk. She told him of unhappy marriages, and he spoke of his very happy one. By summer's end, they married and enjoyed five happy years together, both very glad he had survived the war and for an opportunity to get it right this time.

As it turned out, even half a century later, she was not as fortunate. Jeannie became one of World War II's final casualties. Working as a riveter fifty years earlier in an asbestos-filled shipyard thousands of miles away from any battlefield caught up with her. But not before she had a second chance with the love of her life.

## VOICE THIRTEEN

## DECEMBER 1944

### "Cheek to Cheek"

### "Buffalo Gals"

J.L. rereads and folds the letter from Jeannie before putting it back in his uniform pocket. Of all the pain and discomfort this war had meted out, the unscented letter's contents wound him more deeply. He understands her situation, but comprehension doesn't make her decision any less painful. After all, he has told her she might not want to wait for him, that although he intends to return, he can't make any guarantees.

From his cramped position within Old Ironsides 63, a tank belonging to the first armored division and his mobile home-away-from-home with the 777th Tank Battalion, John Lewis regrets his decision to enlist.

He needs a cigarette. When the armored vehicle comes to a stop and the hatch is opened, J.L. climbs out with the crew for a smoke.

Harry carves his fourth Kilroy in as many days on the single remaining wall of a shelled building. Surrounded by G.I. jokes and laughter, J.L.'s mind is elsewhere. One-handed, he flips open the Zippo and holds the lighter to the unfiltered cigarette. Sucking the flame into the paper, he closes his eyes to keep the smoke from watering his eyes as the tobacco ignites, warming his lungs. J.L. exhales and takes a step forward to retrieve the retreating smoke a second time into his lungs. Tears burn his eyes.

It wasn't idealism or romantic notions of war that compelled him to sign up. His own father served in the Great War and shared stories of mustard gas and trench warfare. A Purple Heart rested atop the bureau in the dining room in a velvet box. He thinks of the pictures his mother and sis had taken of them before he left, his dad in his still-fitting wool breeches and uniform blouse from the Great War next to J.L. in his olive, woolen winter-dress uniform.

J.L. settles back as the heady rush from the last of his five-cent–a-pack nicotine stick subsides. He takes another long drag. The ring of fire burns his fingers, and he pitches the butt to the ground and blows smoke through his nose. Not allowing the chain to be broken, he rolls a cigarette and pinches a loose piece of tobacco from his tongue.

J.L. gives the appearance of attentiveness, but his mind is on a stash of letters. J.L. has amassed a sizable stack of correspondence that he adds to and binds tightly with twine to conserve space. This last, which began John Dear, rests in his breast pocket behind the soft-pack of Camel straights. The irony of her form of address is not lost on him.

As the smoke break ends, the crew attends to the routines of life about the tracked vehicle they called home. J.L. conducts his ordnance inventory. She will always love him, her blue ink says.

The tank begins to roll, pitching over the uneven terrain. He thinks of their last time together, dancing to "Cheek to Cheek," and drifts off despite the constant jostling of the armored vehicle. He's grown used to its rough cadence.

Despite the fitful nature of sleep in the confines of a shared space with other men, their noises and their smells, J.L. is thankful he isn't still on foot. Together with hundreds of newly arrived troops, J.L. had marched 109 miles within the first three days of their arrival to find their place on the front row of the European theater. Blistered and numb from the cold, J.L. had billeted for a time in the home of a family with a beautiful daughter. The girl didn't speak a word of English but played the accordion fluently. Harry wooed her with his rudimentary piano skills, producing a passable "Buffalo Gals," on the concertina.

As they advance in the Ardennes Forest, J.L. regrets that he had not been able to convey his feelings for Jeannie. J.L. lacks the words to adequately express the brutal experiences of his winter trek through the bitter landscape, a redaction she had mistaken for a cooling of affection. But his heart is broken. U.S. Steel-plated armor and artillery protect his body against incoming mortar rounds during their sojourn through the Belgian forest.

As J.L. and thousands of others face the brutality that is the Bulge, her words wound him; this letter will be her last. She asks him to dispose of any letters from her. It will be easier that way, she promises.

Huddled in the belly of the tank, J.L. figures she is right. There is nothing further to be said. The first chance he has, J.L. touches the tongue of the Zippo to the bundled words. Flames follow the string holding the paper together and J.L. tosses released promises on a smoldering ash heap. Nearby, using a detached bayonet, Harry etches a figure with a long nose peeking over a wall onto an abandoned German kubelwagen, the Third Reich's version of the Willy's Jeep.

J.L. doesn't have much time for second thoughts as his crew chases retreating Jerries across the thawing tundra toward Leipzig. Life is clocked in hours of boredom tinged by minutes of anxiety punctuated by seconds of seemingly unending terror. J.L. automatically loads rounds of mortar as rapidly as they can be fired. The enemy fires back with equal effectiveness against the Allies with anti-tank guns. For days J.L. feeds the machine that eats through the Nazi defenses. Following a weeklong battle for Leipzig, the 28th Division gains the upper hand.

Heralded as a great feat, a munition capture and subsequent taking of 365 German prisoners of war deliver a hollow victory. One soldier in their unit is picked off by a sniper hiding in a linden tree. Under heavy panzer fire, his buddy Harry, the Kilroy artist, becomes one more casualty of war. Hit by small arms fire, the infantryman is taken prisoner in Leipzig at the Battle of Nations Monument where Napoleon had likewise faced defeat. A stronghold of the Third Reich, the granite fortress serves as Hitler's SS high command post. When the monument falls under the relentless siege by Allied artillery, retreating SS and captive US troops alike are entombed in rubble.

The relentlessness of war drives the 777 deeper into the Rhineland. In the days following the fall of one of Germany's most powerful and populous cities, J.L.'s battalion rolls up to a fenced enclosure in the gray dawn. Inside the gates the regiment discovers a housing unit with 1500 concentrated inside. Emaciated human shells, along with the remains whose time ran out before their rescue, are liberated or buried by Allied troops who discover them in the waning hours of the war.

As an attempt to boost the 777th morale, the U.S.O puts on a show for those who have made it to what promises to be the turning of the war's tide. The Nazi's have retreated, and Bob Hope advanced to the front. Until that time, one of the retreating tactics of the Third Reich has been to follow Hope's tour and launch attacks accordingly to maximize their chances of inflicting greater destruction. The only devastation the night of Hope's appearance happened when he introduced his next song, "Thanks for the Memory" to the broken-hearted. J.L. was not the only man to be wounded thus.

According to the discharge papers following his honorable separation from the United States Army, PFC John Lewis receives two Bronze Stars, an Overseas Bar, an American Theater Ribbon, a World War II Victory Medal, a Good Conduct Medal, and $174.70 for his service in Rhineland Central Europe. J.L. separates from the Army on the Eastern seaboard, where standing in line for his pay, he strikes up a conversation with a guy from his home state. Hap only received $11 in his pay packet. As a ball turret gunner, he figured he had more coming to him, but go figure. With safety in numbers and two thumbs being better than one, the Missouri boys plan to hitch their way home together. Hap figures since he is stiffed of what he was owed, he is entitled to keep the government-issue flight jacket, so he tosses it over the base fence and retrieves it on the other side. The pair hitchhike to Atlantic City where Hap doubles, triples, and then quadruples his money shooting craps. J.L. figures he will be money ahead not taking any chances on games of chance, so he puts all but four dollars of his severance in a Prince Albert tin. Wandering the Boardwalk, J.L. puts two two-dollar bills down on a Kilroy tattoo.

An official looking envelope with the White House as the return address beats J.L. home. Signed by Harry Truman, the letter states: *To you who answered the call of your country and served in its Armed Forces to bring about the total defeat of the enemy, I extend the heartfelt thanks of a grateful Nation. As one of the Nation's finest, you undertook the most severe task one can be called upon to perform. Because you demonstrated the fortitude, resourcefulness and calm judgment necessary to carry out the task, we now look to you for leadership and example to further exalting our country in peace.*

**WE PROUDLY PRESENT**

**JAY L. WHORTON**

**IN HIS OWN WORDS**

*My name is Jay Whorton from Union Star, Missouri. This is the experience I had in the service during World War II. I served in the US Navy in WW II in the South Pacific on a ship the USS Baltimore, a heavy cruiser. We were in the 3rd fleet and Admiral Halsey was fleet commander. The fleet consisted of 125 to 150 ships that could travel 50 miles an hour. Most of the ships were big battleships, heavy cruisers, aircraft carriers, a few destroyers, and submarines at times. The fleet was set up to escort and protect the aircraft carriers. Japan had suicide bomber planes and their main target was our aircraft carriers. They would get so high they were out of reach of our radar as they went into their dive. They dived so fast when we did pick them up that we couldn't track them. We shot at them with a lot of guns, we hit them enough that most of the time they missed their target, and they went into the water. The aircraft carrier was a big ship high above water and had a big flight deck. It carried some fighter planes but mostly planes with bombs on them. They were used to bomb on land and at sea.*

*We had another fleet of ships, the 7th fleet. It was made up of battleships, an older class of ships that traveled slower as they bombarded. This was their main duties, because they were equipped with sixteen-inch, long range guns.*

*My brother, Don Whorton was a signalman, on one of these battleships, the USS West Virginia. After both fleets of ships had been at sea for several months, they dropped anchor for a while along the coast of the Philippine Islands. The crews had a chance to get off the ships on a bare strip of land for a few hours at a time.*

*Don, being a signalman, spotted the ship I was on and signalled the USS Baltimore and set up a time for us to meet on the bare strip of land with a swamp behind it. When I got the message, it was unbelievable and the best news that we were going to see each other and we did, on that bare strip of land a long ways from home. It was great we were together for two hours, one time!*

*Both fleets left there, and the 7th fleet got into battle with the Japanese fleet. They caught them coming through the Sergone Straights and that almost ended the Japanese fleet.*

*The 3d fleet had been in the China Sea for a while, and in December 1944 Admiral Halsey, was in command of the 3rd fleet on the flag ship the USS New Jersey. We were at sea east of the Philippines. I went on watch above deck in the gun room of an enclosed mount with two five-inch guns. Mount number five; that was my battle station. The watch was from 2am to 7am. On watch was a crew to man one gun if necessary. As I went on watch, the sea was rougher than usual. On watch I was to man the phones. We got orders from the bridge from the officer of the day. An hour later conditions were considerably worse, and we had high winds. I called the bridge about the high winds and was told we were heading straight into*

*a typhoon and everybody top side was to go below deck. A line would be put up from the upper handling room below the gun room to the hatch to go below. A safety line in case the wind caught you and you couldn't see. I would get orders for only one at a time to go below. The ship had to get in a position to break the wind. For this reason, it took a long time to get below. A 170 mile an hour wind was out there. We had a hatch that let the crew in the gun room to get down to the upper handling room. While I was waiting in the gun room, at two windbreaks, I opened a small hatch. The first time I saw a wall of green water as high as I could see, and the second we were on top of a wave or swell and it was a long way to the water. I was the last one to go below from mount number five.*

*I got below the deck and went to the mess hall to eat. Crewmen were coming out with their food on a tray heading for a table, but were out of control, slipping, sliding, and falling. They closed down serving and I went to my living quarters where trash cans were rolling and banging, locker doors banging and supplies coming out. Crew members were rolling out of their bunks also. It was impossible to stand without holding on to something.*

*The ship was cracking. When the screws would come out of the water and then they hit the water again the ship would really shake. This went on hour after hour... no let up. I decided the ship had to keep its power. I prayed to God that the ship would keep its power and give the navigators the ability to steer the ship so it would stay afloat. That was the only way we would stay afloat. That was the only way we would get through the typhoon alive. We never lost our power, and the navigators did the rest. The typhoon was an act of God, and it was an act of God most of us got through it alive. We were in the typhoon for 27 hours with no one top side for 17 hours and the ship was rolling 46 degrees, near the limit. Three ships sank and the crews went down with them. Thousands lost their lives. The hardest thing for me to deal with during the war was going through the typhoon.*

*Halsey, the commander of the 3rd fleet took the fleet of ships right straight into the typhoon, over a chance he had to turn the fleet and get away from it. A fleet of ships with army troops aboard was heading for the Philippines, with the typhoon between them and the Philippines. They turned away from it. They were several days longer getting to the Philippines. The Pacific Ocean is big, and when you're out there it is 13 miles to the horizon. When the 3rd fleet was in formation the ships were 20 miles apart. So we had plenty of room to get away from the typhoon. Shortly after the typhoon, Admiral Halsey lost command of the 3rd fleet.*

*Admiral Nimitz took command, and the fleet went from the 3rd fleet to the 5th fleet. He was in command till the end of the war. April of 1945 was the beginning of the invasion of Okinawa, the* biggest island in the South Pacific. On a clear day with no wind the 5th fleet ran into high waves. The ship USS Quincy, a heavy cruiser, went down under one of those waves and as it came up, 102 feet of its bow broke off. The bow stayed afloat and was tied on to the front of the ship and the ship backed down to Guam. The ship's bow was damaged by a typhoon that caused it to break off.

We had been at general quarters about all day when a suicide plane got in on us that our radar didn't pick up and made a direct hit on the USS Franklin, the newest and the biggest aircraft carrier afloat. A Japanese plane dropped four bombs as the plane hit. The ship was filled with black smoke from front to back. I saw it as I trained the mount on it. Almost all the crew was lost and the ship badly damaged. We went on and I didn't know what happened to the ship. The 7th fleet was there along the coast of Okinawa and the USS West Virginia, the ship my brother Don was on, took a bomb that went down into the laundry room and didn't go off. A Lieutenant took Don down where the bomb was and took the fuse out of it. The invasion of Okinawa was progressing toward the end in July 1945.

In August of 1945 the big secret of WWII was two atom bombs that were located at Guam and put on a plane. The first one was dropped August 6th on Hiroshima and the second one dropped on Nagasaki August 9th. This was the beginning of the end of WWII.

One more mission had to happen; a fleet of ships was to go to Tokyo to sign a peace treaty. The USS Baltimore was to be one of those ships, but the Baltimore was condemned unable to go because of the damage done by the typhoon.

On September 2, 1945, four countries arrived on board the USS Missouri, a battleship, anchored in Tokyo Bay to sign the surrender papers. Gen Douglas Macarthur signed for the United States. The other countries were Germany, England, and Japan.

The United States was involved in the war all over the world. During my service I was awarded 6 bronze stars: Asiatic Pacific: 4 stars, Philippines Liberation: 1 star, and Occupation of Japan: 1 star.

At the end of the war the USS Baltimore was repaired from the typhoon damage. The USS Baltimore and its crew were assigned to the occupation of Japan, and we were to spend six months there. We had four places to go: 1" Kure Bay, 21 Hiroshima, 3d Nagasaki, and 4th Tokyo. Our reason for going there was to destroy war weapons, shells, and guns. We found building after building full of guns. We had guard duty and cleaned up.

Hiroshima was where the first atom bomb was dropped. I took this picture of a Japanese man at the site of the bomb and the damage of what the bomb did. He could speak English and he told me it killed everyone that came there two weeks after the bomb was dropped. You can see from the picture nothing is left. We moved on down the coast to Nagasaki, the place where the second atom bomb was dropped. I took a picture, and it shows the remains of a prison that was reported the prison General Wainwright and his troop were in. The first atom bomb dropped

August 6, 1945, and the second dropped August the 9th, Later I found that Wainwright and his troops were captured at Baton in the Philippines in 1942 and were in the Baton death march and later put in prison at Manchuria China and released August 20th, 1945.

The USS Baltimore and its crew moved down the coast to Tokyo, the 4th and last stop of the occupation of Japan. On our way from the south Pacific to the occupation of Japan, Baltimore was asked to organize two baseball teams to play when we got to Tokyo. On the ship they had the equipment to play with. A diamond was to be made in Tokyo for us to play on. Johnnie Visinaskic was asked to be the player manager of one of the teams. Johnnie asked Mark Maralingki, me and nine others all from the same division to play on one of the teams. I played 2nd base. Twelve from another division made up the other team. The diamond and park was built and ready for us to play when we got to Tokyo. The two ball teams came ashore in Tokyo to play, and we were greeted with a big crowd. They knew we were coming. It was a special occasion for them to be there. They came to see us play the first baseball game ever to be played on Japanese soil. The game was new to them, and we played the nine positions to the best of our ability. To see a baseball game was great entertainment for them as the crowd got bigger every game. They were thrilled at every play and every game. John Woerle, my shipmate, took the pictures that day. The first picture was as we started to the diamond and then we changed rolls, with six pictures on a roll. He took pictures of the ballpark, people in the grandstand and the players. These pictures didn't develop, or they got lost. I didn't develop the pictures until I got back to the states. The Japanese people all over Tokyo were so kind and friendly to the service men for us being there.

General MacArthur oversaw the occupation of Japan. He worked with the Emperor and stayed in the Emperor's palace that was on top of a hill and consisted of 500 acres surrounded by a channel of water.

When I had guard duty I stood guard at the entrance gate to the palace, the only gate. I took this picture of the channel. MacArthur would come through that gate every morning as he had an office a few blocks from there in Tokyo. They came through the gate in three American cars with flags on them, a one-star General in the front car, MacArthur, a five star in the middle car and a one-star General in the back car. The Japanese men and women and children lined up on both sides of the street by the hundreds. As the cars went by, they stood at attention and saluted. They showed they honored him and liked him very much.

I was in Tokyo one day and a group of US Army men crossed behind me and soon someone called my name. I looked around *and saw Kenton Ebersold from Union Star Mo, the same town I was from with a big smile on his face. I was very surprised to see him, and that someone knew me a long way from home.*

*Kenton was stationed and camped in the hills outside of Tokyo. Kenton duty in Tokyo that day and we had a short time to visit. Kenton and his Army buddies told me while in the hills they decided to form and piece together their own church service. An Army buddy told me Kenton led the church service. Kenton came from the Philippines to Japan. I asked him about the typhoon, and he said he was on one of the troop ships that got away from it. He said it took them longer to get to the Philippines.*

*I will always remember taking part in the occupation of Japan serving and being in a foreign country. I got to see General Douglas MacArthur as he worked with the Emperor of Japan to make it a better place to live and recover from the war.*

*The USS Baltimore and its crew's duty came to an end for the occupation of Japan. We were ordered to sail back to the United States and anchored the ship at Brimington, Washington. We ferried to and from Seattle Washington where I had guard duty, and we went over there on a pass. And after a while we got orders to put the ship in inactive duty. This meant that all the compartments were to be cleaned and sealed with five layers of plastic. That's what I did at the end of my service in the US Navy.*

*After the war Don Whorton, Kenton Ebersold, and I returned back to Union Star, Missouri seventy years ago. Don married Georgia Simerly and they became the parents of six children. Kenton married Betty Gibson and they became the parents of six children. I married Hazel Ebersold, Kenton's sister and we became the parents of six children.*

*The eighteen children went to the same school at Union Star Missouri and graduated from Union Star High School, five girls and 13 boys. Many of them still live around Union Star.*

*Three have passed away. Don Whorton: born 7/22/1925 and died 3/16/1983. Kenton Ebersold: born 4/13/1926 and died 9/21/2009 and Kenton and Betty's son Jay Kenton Ebersold: born 9/19/1959 and died 3/13/2010. May God Bless their loved ones. It doesn't seem fair when we lose a loved one, someone near to us and all we have is memories, but that's something we will always have.*

*I am thankful that you let me share this part of my life.*

*I am proud to be your husband, your father, your father-in-law, your grandfather, your great grandfather, your brother, your brother-in-law, your uncle, your great uncle. I am thankful for my relation.*

*Jay L. Whorton*

*born February 27, 1924*

Jay Loyd Whorton, 97, St. Joseph, Missouri, formerly of Union Star, Missouri, passed away Friday, November 26, 2021.

He was born February 27, 1924, in Helena, Missouri to Basil and Lois (Dorrel) Whorton.

Jay married Hazel Iris Ebersold on June 9, 1946. She preceded him in death on May 24, 2019.

He was a member of the United States Navy, serving in World War II in the South Pacific aboard the USS Baltimore as a gunner's mate. He was a part of the occupation of Japan as a guard to the Emperor's Palace.

For 52 years, Jay was a farmer and active in the Union Star community and church. He grew up farming with horses, fishing, and trapping.

Jay enjoyed time with his family, John Deere tractors, and playing and watching sports, especially baseball.

Jay J Whorton

Japanese lined up to go see us play their first baseball game

The Japanese man I talked to
Cleveland emperor's palace
at Tokyo

Don W Whorton

Kenton Ebersold

## VIGNETTE FOURTEEN

## JANUARY 1st

### "Auld Lang Syne"

"Penelope, that's her name? The lady who made these pierogies and heads up the All-Saints team that wins the 'Pierogi of the Parish Cookoff' every year, that's Penelope?" asked an incredulous Hannah from behind the newspaper. At 17, Hannah couldn't fathom that Mrs. D'Angelo, that ancient woman, had ever been her age. She did have to admit any time she heard her speak it was with a trace of English accent, which she thought was kind of cool. And she made wonderful pierogies. Hannah put down the newspaper.

"Mrs. D'Angelo. Yes, that's the one," said her father, Steve, setting down his cup of coffee. "Grew up on an estate in Yorkshire that her dad managed. Met her husband in England during World War II, married, and came to live in the U.S." Steve wrote for the local paper and had written the feature his daughter had just read.

Robin put down her buttered toast, brushed her hands of crumbs, and picked up the newspaper to take a look for herself. "I have to admit, I always see her more as the Dowager Countess than Lady Sibyl," she offered. Robin was a huge *Downton Abbey* fan. "But maybe that's just because she's been old for as long as I've known her."

"Or more Queen Elizabeth than Princess Margaret," added Hannah, who had just finished the last season of *The Crown* with her mother and always loved Margaret's defiant spirit. It was her first but her mother's third time through the series.

"I don't think either is an entirely valid analogy," said her father. "It would be more like if Anna married a stable groom rather than Bates and they had a daughter who had the run of the Crawley estate who then grew up to marry an American G.I."

"And since when did you become so well versed in the fictional world of Julian Fellowes?" Robin laughed. "I thought you thought it was all "so much melodramatic British soap opera.'"

Steve shrugged. "What can I say, you've watched it so many times, some of it is bound to rub off."

"Well, she's famous for her pierogies, so it's just like if Daisy and William had a kid. And William hadn't died from the war," Hannah insisted with more excitement than she intended.

"Well, not exactly. William was in World War I and a Tommy, a British soldier, so wrong war, wrong country, but yeah, I guess that's closer," Steve conceded. "Her mother was a governess to the family and not Mrs. Patmore. Half French. Her grandmother had been an au pair in Paris for the daughter of the little girl who inspired *Alice in Wonderland*," he explained, realizing the absurdity of relating a PBS Masterpiece series and what he assumed Hannah would think was just some old Disney movie. The actual, living, breathing fascinating woman he had interviewed for the piece was so much more than a geriatric woman known for her potato dumplings. "She's really far more interesting than all that claptrap on TV. But, you mentioned *The Crown*, her parents received a telegram from Queen Elizabeth on their diamond wedding." Then to impress his daughter that he was down with her slang he added, "For reals."

Hannah didn't bite. "You're kidding me? The Queen, the one who died, congratulated some random old couple?" Hannah asked.

"They were her subjects. And not everyone stays married for 60 years," Steve explained.

"Or even live that long," Robin added. "'Subjects' sounds so colonial, by the way."

"Well, that's what they were up until the 80s," he said, "Subjects of the realm."

"Off with their heads!" Hannah joked.

"So you do know what *Alice in Wonderland* is!" her father said. "I'm proud of you."

"I do go to school, Dad," the teen said, rolling her eyes. "But as far as queens go, Mom, remember that episode of *The Crown* when they snuck out of Buckingham Palace? Why was that such a big deal?"

"It was V-E day," her dad answered for her mom. "Allegedly a true story."

"That would have been so fun," Hannah sighed. "To get out of the house and away from her parents for once."

"Oh, like you don't have fun. Speaking of fun, did you kiss anyone special last night at midnight?" Robin inquired of the New Year's Eve party her daughter attended with her boyfriend Toby.

"I'll never tell," said the girl, vaguely. "Did you guys even stay awake 'til 12?"

"I'll have you know we saw the ball drop in Times Square, toasted the New Year with some bubbly, and sang 'Auld Lang Syne,'" her mother answered defensively. "Dale Carlton played it on the piano. Who knew? Then we told the Carltons they were welcome to stay, but we were going to bed."

"Here's your hat, what's your hurry," her father confirmed.

"I wonder what old Mrs. D'Angelo did for fun back in her day?" Hannah asked.

"I'm not sure, but these days she joked that her social life consists of going to funerals for her friends," Steve remembered.

"Oh, that sounds fun," said Hannah.

"Might sound dull, but she said they'd been pretty eventful of late. Mrs. D'Angelo told me she recently attended services for this woman she knew for years. Assumed she was American. Turned out the old gal was born in Austria and had been a German spy. But wait–there's more. This woman turned double agent and delivered the goods on Hitler to the Allies. Nobody knew about it until her funeral. Worked undercover as a librarian. Crazy cloak and dagger stuff. Not even sure her husband ever knew. He died years earlier. The rest of her family didn't find out about granny's past until her funeral when she wrote a letter and had the funeral director read it. She lived her entire life having been sworn to secrecy by the O.S.S. Can you imagine?"

"Get outta here," Hannah said.

"And, get this, the woman who died, she and Mrs. D'Angelo had a mutual friend who lived to be over a 100. Except something about she was born on a leap year so calendar-wise was only 20-something. At THAT woman's funeral, her great grandson played a song that his great grandfather had written about her during the war. They found the sheet music to this waltz or polka or something with her name as the title. Helen of Troy, I think she said. Anyway, that gal was a spy too, as was her husband. You can't make this stuff up."

"Do you think Mrs. D'Angelo was telling the truth about her friends or is she a little batty?" Hannah asked, twirling her finger by her ear.

"All I know is that's what she told me. Hey, pass the pierogies," Steve said.

## VOICE FOURTEEN

## LONDON, JANUARY 1945

Poppy had grown so tired of her brown plaid wool jumper and could hardly wait for Easter when their family might have accrued enough garment coupons to purchase a new outfit. Food rationing had at least assured her clothing still fit after a solid year with nary a new frock, but it was so demoralizing to be 18 and seen dressed the same at every event. So to school, choir practice, or the pictures, it made no difference where she was. Sartorially it was all the same.

At least she was not alone in this. Her chums suffered a similar fate. She supposed she had the blackout to be thankful for. As they lived most of their public lives in the dark, no one was the wiser. Still, she ached for something blue, red, or green, in taffeta, velvet, or silk, and longed not to have to accessorize with the compulsory gas mask handbag she was sentenced to always carry with her.

She knew the world wasn't really conspiring to ruin her youth, but she rather hoped girls in other countries were making similar sacrifices. Then she would chastise herself for wallowing in self-pity and get on with it. But dressed in items from her austere wardrobe, Poppy remembered better days when her family lived at the woodsy estate at Lyme Park. She sketched the fashions she saw in magazines and imagined better days ahead. She treasured the colored pencils her brother gave her for Christmas and filled the book of blank pages she found at a jumble sale with drawings of girls in fantastical gowns wearing satin slippers.

It was during these stolen hours that Poppy felt especially close to Edward, her older brother who was in the Merchant Navy. She and Edward had once watched a bi-plane sputter and spiral to a field filled with deer. One deer that lived in the deer park was her special pet. He was remarkable for only having one antler. The Aldridges for whom both their parents worked had been forced to turn the gated estate over to the National Trust early in the war and the military took over

Lyme Park. As the grand house and the adjacent cottages now housed officers, it had become necessary for the Burnhams to relocate to a rented flat in London for work.

She missed Patch, their little fox terrier, but she positively agonized over Edward's absence. One day they were watching for the occasional simple flying machine to soar over the estate, and the next day the skies were filled with malevolent machines on sinister missions. Edward had joined up, in effect leaving her a homeless only child dressed in dowdy sameness and with no dog to run and play with and no place to do so if she had one.

Life on the estate was so full of music, liveliness, and color. Her Pa-Pa and the gamekeepers who raised pheasants for the hunts or worked in the stables like her father would play fiddles as Mummy and the women who worked downstairs would dance a jig, clap and sing.

Then one day as Mummy was riding a bicycle into Disley to visit the grocer an automobile struck her. She recovered, but her employment prospects were limited to taking in wash for those who could afford to pay her, while Pa-Pa spent most of his time at the docks, working extra shifts. With Edward away learning shipboard radio operations, Poppy listened to radio broadcasts that spelled near disaster for those trapped at Dunkirk.

Needing a distraction, Poppy became active in the church choir. The young people who gathered each Wednesday evening to sing, would do so under the cover of darkness. Poppy loved singing and was especially fond of "Be Thou My Vision," which they were to perform for Easter. The line "Heart of my own heart, whatever befall, Still be my vision, O ruler of all" especially resonated with her. Between the threat of buzz bombs and air raids, "Whatever befall" seemed to apply to every aspect of her life.

One night at choir practice, her friend Audrey told her of a dance being held two days hence, on Friday. Both girls lamented the state of their clothing options and decided to trade outfits for the occasion. Neither would be dressed in anything new, but what each wore would at least be new to each girl. Poppy felt like a brand-new girl in Audrey's gray and maroon dress. She slept in pin curls and pinched her cheeks in preparation for the evening. As she left, her mother told her to be home by 10. She would worry anyway about Poppy making her way home in the dark since taking a torch was not an option. Poppy was used to her mother's "Nothing good happens after ten" frequent refrain.

Entering the hall, the girls were excited and a little frightened to see so many soldiers in attendance. When one brash American G.I. approached Audrey, he handed her a Coca-Cola and complimented her on her dress. Poppy had to hide her laughter, knowing he couldn't be serious as it was her dress and one she despised. She had heard the Americans were bold, but she sensed the blonde-haired poster boy for Uncle Sam was sincere in his admiration of her dress on her best friend.

Another G.I. joined the trio, but hardly said a word. The band played a swing number, Poppy's favorite, and Audrey and her G.I., whose last name was Beauregard, took to the floor, leaving Poppy to stand with the other soldier.

Over the music, he said, "Hitler banned this music, you know." Poppy did not know this, but it made her love the song all the more. She looked more closely at the soldier, noticing behind his glasses just how light his brown eyes were for someone with such dark hair and olive skin.

"D'Angelo, Robert D'Angelo," he said.

In a joking humor, she replied, "Burnham, Penelope Burnham."

He laughed, "Fair enough. Friends call me Bobby."

"Friends call me Poppy," she answered.

"Well, which will it be," he countered, "Penelope or Poppy?"

"That has yet to be determined, Robert D'Angelo," she answered, looking away to hide her smile.

Several minutes passed as Audrey and Beau danced. "Say, will you give me your address, Miss Penelope?" he asked, pulling his copy of the Soldiers and Sailors Prayer book from his uniform pocket. This was an unexpected turn of events, and cheeky though he was, she was glad for his boldness in asking, so she took the book and offered eraserless pencil and recorded her name, *Miss Penelope Burnham*. But in a moment of trepidation, she wrote down her former address on the estate. She was never going to see this man again, so what did it matter that she preferred for him to think she had a more impressive address than her current residence. Poppy closed the book and handed it to him. He slipped it into his pocket without looking at it.

Over the music and with one eye on their friends, D'Angelo told the girl he was in the Air Corps, having always loved planes. A desk jockey rather than a pilot due to his eyesight. He told her of a scrapbook he kept as a boy, cutting out and pasting page after page of airplane pictures that he then drew and designed little models for. She lost a bit of her reserve and told him of her sketches of dresses and that her brother, Edward, was a radio operator at sea. He had a sister named Maria and a calico cat called Peaches. She used to have a dog named Patch who would hide under the bed any time a squadron of airplanes flew over.

He worked out of an office on Grosvenor Street and had the use of a four-speed Vauxhall, which was not bad for a boy whose people were first generation Italian American. His mother made the world's best pierogies. She enjoyed being out of doors and would finish school in May, at which time her friend Audrey's father had secured her a position as a telephone switchboard operator. They both hated Hitler and stewed tomatoes and thought their country's respective leader was the world's best.

Suddenly the bandleader leaned into the microphone stand and announced a dance contest. The orchestra kicked into "G.I. Jive." "They're playing my song," D'Angelo shouted as he took her by the hand and pulled her onto the dance floor. A judge circled the floor, tapping to eliminate couples as the jive gave way to "Sing, Sing, Sing."

In between a Gene Krupa and a Benny Goodwin song, the band leader told the dancers he once heard Captain Glenn Miller salute the guys who have the rear flank of every fighter formation with "The Tail-End Charlies." He then led his orchestra to perform the War Department V-Disc sensation, followed by the flip side, "String of Pearls." Two by two, the dance floor emptied until only four couples remained. Audrey and the chiseled-jaw blond Yank and Poppy and Robert D'Angelo among them.

By the time the band broke into "In the Mood," pairs swung and swayed while the more serious contenders dodged the dance judge. Audrey and her beau, who had been jitterbugging, fox trotting, and Lindy Hopping all evening, were pooped from what was becoming a marathon. No match for the heartier die-hards, the two retreated of their own volition to the table where a by-now lukewarm Coca-Cola waited.

Thinking they were the next to be nixed, Poppy and D'Angelo saw the dance judge reach for them. But instead of tapping them to sit out, he grabbed them each by the hand and raised their arms, pre-emptively declaring them the winners and dismissing the runners up. Her partner bowed and said, "Thank you for the dance, Miss Penelope."

A crowd of fellow soldiers swarmed D'Angelo with congratulations, patting him on the back and celebrating, further evidence theirs was the winning side. The band leader took to the mic to say they would be awarding their prize at the end of the night. Noticing the late hour, Poppy was hit by a sudden panic. "I have to get home, Bobby," she said. "I had a lovely time." Then she dashed for the door, pulling Audrey in her wake before any trophy could be handed out.

Bobby D'Angelo wasn't worried. The next day he asked around for the girl in the gray and maroon dress who had been his dance partner. The only person who seemed to recognize a girl matching that description said he didn't know her name, but the warden was positive it wasn't Penelope or Poppy.

D'Angelo, remembering she had written her address in his prayer book, wrote her a letter. One day an envelope arrived but it was the one he had posted, stamped return to sender as no one by that name lived at Lyme Park. The former residents, the Aldridge family, most certainly would have recognized the name Penelope Burnham but even they no longer lived on the estate.

So it was with a dejected heart that this seeming Cinderella would never be found that D'Angelo attended a church service on Easter morning. From her position on the back row in the choir, an alto in a blue velvet dress sang "Be Thou My Vision." Spying Bobby slumped on the back pew, her heart began to race, almost signaling her whereabouts, for just then he lifted his bespectacled eyes to the choir loft. He smiled and sat up. She determined then and there to speak to him after the service and ask if he would like to see her sketches. Throw caution to the wind. And maybe even tell him to call her "Poppy". She could be cheeky too.

She did not yet know that in the coming days her beloved Edward's Royal Fleet Auxiliary ship would be torpedoed by a German U-boat. Her parents have yet to receive the letter from the Ministry of War Transport stating with regret that 2nd Radio Officer Edward Burnham "has been recorded missing, presumed drowned, whilst in service of his ship." The last line of the letter would assure them that their son "worthily upheld the noble traditions of the Merchant Navy" and that "the realisation of that fact might help soften the heavy blow which has fallen upon you."

While those words would be appreciated, they would offer little balm for the pain of losing Edward. Still, the family would treasure the kind words spoken of their beloved son and brother.

For now, Poppy just knew it will be a comfort to have the friendship of this kind American, Bobby D'Angelo, whatever befalls.

###

## Afterward

I am so grateful for those of you who shared stories and photographs for *Victory Vignettes & Voices*. Although the book is presented as a novel and many of the stories are fictionalized, very real people informed the writing. However, unless otherwise noted, characters are composites and events are presented as fiction based on historical facts, details, and stories. Nearly every line is based on a depiction or description that someone shared with me and in many cases (especially Vignette Nine), the narrative is a compilation of anecdotes from several sources.

This book developed foremost out of a deep appreciation and respect for the men and women who served our country during World War II. A record number of veterans are lost each day, thus the urgency to record their stories. Fortunately, we still have recordings of the musicians, singers, and composers who brought us the endearing and enduring music we associate with this Greatest Generation. That music and the Steinway initiative to build G. I. pianos to boost morale created a unifying theme. Learn more about the Victory Vertical Project online. Don't miss the interview by Garik Pedersen with the late Henry Z. Steinway, during which Steinway said of all their achievements, his family was proudest of the Victory Vertical project.

burial, arriving Monday night. Mrs. Enos Taylor, mother of Mrs. Sherard, who with her husband went to Kentucky to be with them when the baby came, remained with her daughter and will bring her home later when she is able to travel.

The father Pfc. Ronald Sherard was at the hospital when the baby arrived, but left two hours afterward for overseas service and has not yet learned of its death. The sympathy

St. Louis, Mo. for discharge. This was accomplished Mar 3, 1946. Dad, Mom & Wava Ellen were there to pick me up and get back to Maysville. This was three years I had not anticipated to happen in my life an Experience I Never forgot.

YANKS IN REICH . . . Boxes locate areas where eight United States army divisions have been assigned to duty in the American zone of occupation in Germany. The locations are not necessarily permanent.

ridgefields . . next morning we went up and had to fire. That was on Sunday. We took 35,11 one pure. and 368 prisoners. We then went to Peguu. From there to Borna. Took ... house digging and ... ... prisoners of war. Went back to Borna that night and started to Leipsig. It was all night there. We took the town of Lubertwolkwitz. And Then Took ...

**p. 65 Thomas and Nadyne Jurjevich** (contributed by Mark Justin)

**p. 73 Ronald and Wava Ellen Sherard** (contributed by Joy Sherard); **Hap Echterling,** ball turret gunner on *U.S.S. Manila Bay* (contributed by Cathy Green)

**p. 79 Theodore H. Schoon** (contributed by Sharon Carrol)

**p. 165 Photos clockwise from top left**: Jim Strong (contributed by Donna Gaines), Dwayne Fagan (contributed by Kevin Fagan), Tommy and Carol Sue Taylor, Thomas and Nadyne Jurjevich (contributed by Mark Justin), Eyeglasses (contributed by Kevin Fagan), J.L. "Pete" Peters and friends at table (contributed Janie Christensen), Glenn Miller Autograph (contributed by Tommy Taylor), Bud Strong and island girl (contributed by Donna Gaines), center photo James "Jim" Jambor (contributed by Donna Gaines.)

**p. 166 Photo strip left, from top**: Capt. Gladys Walsh (contributed by Beth Whalen Moutray), J.L. Peters and tank crew (contributed by Janie Christensen), J.L. Peters (contributed by the late Doris Peters), Song and Service book, Bible, and address book belonging to Cpl.Ted Schoon (contributed by Sharon Carrol), Sgt. Francis Schaefer [Purple Heart recipient] (contributed by Jan Burnham Schwarz). Right: John Lewis Peters [Purple Heart recipient] and son J.L. (Janie Christensen), stature of Mary and infant Jesus (contributed by Beth Whalen Moutray), Cameron Veterans Memorial bricks; Merle Green and Texas Ranger crew (Merle Green)

**p. 167 Photos clockwise from top left:** "Bertha, Verna, and Verlin" (contributed by Robert Sigrist, Jack Gaines (contributed by Donna Jambor Gaines), Bud and Jim Strong (contributed by Donna Jambor Gaines), Burma Shave ad, Letter from Harry S. Truman (from the personal effects of J.L. "Pete" Peters), Roi Tan cigar box, postcards, funeral program, wire-rimmed glasses (from the personal effects of Dwayne Fagan), Jim Jambor (contributed by Donna Jambor Gaines) Burma-Shave ad, Merle Green on a South Pacific Island.

**p. 168** Authors maternal and paternal grandparents, Johann "John" and Doris Weidinger (car) and from right--Paul, Maxine, Earl Thomas and Charles Frederick Christensen (author's father, age five). Wall Drug sign in Europe. Airplane pictures and other images from the scrapbook pages of Dwayne Fagan in the 1930s and 40s (author's father-in-law).

**p.169 Photos clockwise from top left:** Merle Green, Memorial Brick, Ronald Sherard, Ronald Sherard Journal (contributed by Joy Sherard), J.L. Peter's journal, St. Joseph Gazette clipping among J.L. Peter's effects saved by his parents, John Weidinger, Newspaper clipping (contributed by Joy Sherard)

Made in the USA
Monee, IL
16 March 2024

54629343R00102